'Bout Time

*With love to Joan
from Joan
5/2/11*

'Bout Time

By Joan Southgate

Eagle Creek Press
Solon, Ohio

©2007 by Joan Southgate
All rights reserved, including the right of reproduction in whole or in any form.
Printed in the United States of America.

Eagle Creek Press
32513 Seneca Drive
Solon, OH 44139

ISBN: 978-0-9759366-5-8

Printed by BookMasters Inc., of Mansfield, Ohio.

*For my mother,
Evelyn Claracy Harris*

I lose time.

Whole blocks of time, while I am still here. I know it only after the fact, after I slowly return. There is a thought, Oh. I am coming back now. I look up. Here I am. I have been away. I am never sure of how long. I sometimes note how long it seems.

Prologue

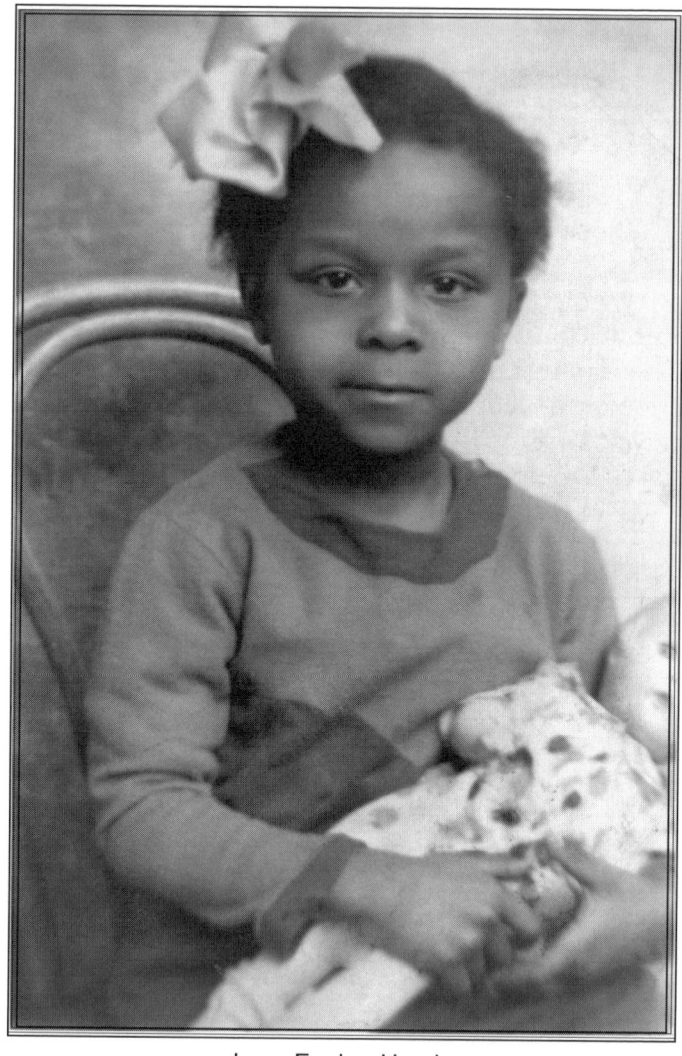

Joan Evelyn Harris
(1934)

Take a friend's hand in both of mine lean back twirl fast faster with all of our might until we both let our hands slip away.

We played statues because it was a good twist to plain old tag, especially if we were bored. Spun round and around until flung out to stop as a stone still statue that should not move or I would lose. The more crooked the shape my body settled into, the greater my skill at the game. Back then all grammar school kids came home at noon to sit at the kitchen table for lunch with the Helen Trent soap opera as radio background. At 12:45 we would hurry back to school- yard lines winding to restless stop at the heavily shellacked, huge wooden doors. The boys pushing and shoving, the girls' line easily more prim.

Walking home at the end of each school day was always the reverse of our morning pick-up. Frances Yvonne was first because she lived practically next door to the school; another few steps, then Marilyn Cox and Mary Lee Page turned right to cross the street and would be home in a second; they were neighbors in the next block; and then me, Norma, Betty (or sometimes Adelaide, much older, who lived on the other side of my house, walking beside us talking together only if our paths happened to cross). We turned left and up the not at all steep hill.

How is it decided which event becomes family jargon?

At the top of Raynor, Betty Glazer and Norma Cohen had to climb the concrete steps of the railway overpass, they left me. I came home from school the same as every other day, and there I stood differently. I know I had said a regular goodbye, but I stopped in space half way between the corner and the path to our house. And that was all. Just me hearing the usual goodbye knowing we would be out to walk again; there wasn't something more I needed to say, no thing I was waiting to hear. Not trying to put an end to some story that would be finished. I stood stopped on the grass, then stayed looking at Adelaide's closed screen door an extraordinarily long time. Was I holding my breath? I did not feel pressed to breathe again, just felt it important to note how long I looked on, untrembling and all right, even when someone else was quickly passing.
    I stood long enough for Mother to hold the kitchen screen door aside and greet me, troubled, What were you looking at, Joan? There wasn't an answer but the words came quick, pleasant and without logic. I was watching Adelaide go into the house. From that day on until we were all very old, any prolonged silence or perhaps day dream, my mother explained away, there's Joan watching Adelaide go in the house.

There is that game we played back then:

If six kids are statues then the seventh is It. We each wait in line to be spun from Its grasp to fly off her fingertips, and land a silent gargoyle lump. Winding unwinding then frozen in space, struck mute so I cannot even join the squealing as I get chosen.

I

I am sixty-three. Two years ago I had the first flashback. Unprecipitated, out of nowhere, crystal clear, and so fast. It was exactly like lightning: no sound, strobe-bright, and absolutely everything could be seen in a moment. Flash!

Too sudden, too complete for any reaction except, Oh.

I am standing in my kitchen. I love warm evenings here. I have this beautiful room that is mine because I thought it up. I built the open pine shelves, stripped and stained the washstands and woodwork. I rubbed the one hundred-fifty-year-old table's patina smooth. I am holding a floral thin china cup of herbal Red Zinger and the real view of my own backyard through the oversized, deep-set, garden window. Suddenly I discover an amnesia so specific that no one noticed it was there while it was happening. And I begin to know what is inside.

It is all carefully sorted in my head. There is: What I lived and remember or sometimes simply forget (Oh yeah, that's right. I forgot).

And there is what has been buried for fifty-six years in a quiet white amnesia and
>Now is
>Clear and sometimes
>Just here.

Each found image surrounds with its own temper. Not every one is terror. Inside my mind I hold it all in layers, but I wish for a vocal asterisk, or perhaps an automatic yellowed voice so that any scene that is brand-new will be plainly marked within my conversation

My father died thirty years ago.

My life began with the 1929 Great Depression. I grew up and went to college in my hometown, graduate school away. I got married old (28) to Robert, who was older (36). I was 31 years old when we had our first child (and we had been trying to get pregnant for 3 years). Our four kids were born into the 1960s civil rights revolution and helped decorate protest signs before they could print their own names. They have grown into bright, kind, splendid adults because a lot of my mother is in my mothering. My mother defined my world by filling it with sound: poem, song, plans for adventure, and significant silence: of questions unanswered. Naming on her own terms, redefining what did not fit, she created the world I grew up in. I thought her sound was universal.

She woke us in the morning singing: Up Up ye lads and lasses gay, to the meadows trip away to the meadow to the meadow trip away. Whenever I sang this old English ditty to my young children, I was singing mostly to myself. It was mother's song to wake me, so I did not use it often for my own kids, instead, after reading their story, I made up a good night singing ritual to put Martha, Robbie, Tisha and Dan down safely into their beds. To the tune of Brahms' Lullaby I would softly creak my voice through, Go to sleep Martha dear (or Robbie or Tisha or Danny) close your little brown eyes, in the morning when you wake you will: Go play in the mud; Swim in the bathtub; Go to the zoo; Tie your shoes again, all by yourself... Every night I would fill in the last line current for each child, followed by required kisses-with-names. I would announce the name and place the kiss on a soft brown cheek. Yabba Dabba Doo Kiss. A Kiss from Me to You Kiss. I Love You Yea Yea Yea Kiss. And a Good Night, Sweet Dreams Kiss. Everyone got all of the kisses. Some nights they suggested names for temporary, delaying kisses that I would give amidst muffled giggles. I did not want to leave, any more than they wanted me to be gone.

 Now, on visits a few times a year, I sit on a small wooden rocking chair that belonged to my mother's tiny mother. Holding another young child, I get to place all of the kisses on soft sweet cheeks, all over again.

 Just like when your father was a little boy.
 Just like when your mother was a little girl.
 Grandma, just like me?
 Yep.

I love watching the exchange between young fathers and tiny children in the doctor's waiting room or on the St. Clair bus. The modern parent treats this intimacy with a dailyness that pretends fathers have been doing this for generations, but that is not true. When I was four, children would not have been taken to doctors' appointments by their fathers, and if someone saw us on the bus with our father, my baby sister Tish and I would have been in velveteen dresses with hand-crocheted Irish lace collars and black patent shoes, my big brothers Shurley and Winthrop in Eton jackets and caps, because this would have had to be a special outing.

I was born about six months before the 1929 market crash and grew up in the debris. My father would (jokingly) say that I caused The Depression. Looking back, he probably truly believed that I had somehow caused his depression. I was the third child, first daughter born to this bright, talented, college-educated artist. An outstanding Negro who was a-credit-to-his-race and before October 1929 was about to move his young family to a position of prestige and money in New York City. At the end of the year, white men were leaping from high office windows because of drastic change in their fortunes. We were black, our fortune changed, the New York City job fell through, and my father did not throw himself out of our window. My father stayed in Syracuse for the rest of his life and made a living as an artist. Some years he made money, some years we were poor. I think he never felt he was a success. Not a success! An American fate worse than death.

He was a young man on the rise, head of a picture-book family, bright, talented, creative, respected. Falstaff Lionel Harris, first Negro to win Syracuse University College of Fine Arts' Leavenworth prize. First Negro to have his studio in a Syracuse business district. First Negro to win this business contract, that private commission. But first-Negro-to was the wrong reference point. My father wanted New York City. He wanted to be with those black artists celebrating the joyful power of the glorious Harlem Renaissance.

My mother was not a hugging kissing affectionate woman but I always felt touched. I don't remember missing her kisses. I can feel her warmth; she must have worked it in without fanfare while she showed us how to do things. How to hold the dust pan, how to knit, crochet, memorize a poem and recite it. How to be polite. And my mother taught us to laugh.

My mother used to say: There's a difference between homely and ugly; in her tone you knew homely was best, sometimes some people are so homely they are beautiful. Like lovely Mary McLeod Bethune? And we both knew that the singer Paul Robeson was just plain handsome: look at the dark color of his skin. Handsome. And brilliant.

Mother used to say: Don't be foolish.

Mother used to say: No.

Mother used to encourage: Keep plugging.

Mother sometimes said, Monkey peanuts,

Dirty Gerty, Rosie the Red, or Ash Can Sally, without explaining she called them that. If we had known, we could have distinguished her lexicon from the words outside where less poetry was spoken.

Mother used to tell us stories, sometimes Ghost Stories, hometown legend that became truth. Scary ghost stories without making us truly afraid. These ghosts just were things that happened, that's the way it was, on any plain old average day, when she was a little girl, living in her house at 48 Fitch Avenue, Auburn N.Y., where my grandmother, her mother, still lived. Mother would sit down and start with sweet low hum-chanting, then slowly, she'd call in the words.

> She'd begin:
> Early one morning [plop plop plop: the sound of slow-moving horse hoof beat]
> Death come a knocking at my door,
> Errr liiee one morning [plip plip plop]
> Death come knocking at my daw uh uh or.

> She'd continue the story:
> There was this man, Mr. Johnson, of the Auburn Johnsons, walking along down Fitch Avenue, heard horse hoof beats pounding a death rattle right up behind him, keeping time steady as you please. And it was early morning 'cause he was on his way to work at the rope factory (where they take hemp and weave it into big old cables strong enough to pull an ocean liner, where my

mother worked herself when she was a young eighteen years old, before she got married to my father.)

And when Mr. Johnson turned around to look where he thought the milkman's wagon was coming right up behind him. Not a soul was on the road. Only him. All by himself. Walking. He didn't even have a carriage or wagon of his very own. He was scared, it was early, still-dark-morning early. And he was all alone but he ran and tried to shake it off and stopped running before he got to work. He did not want any of his friends to think he'd seen a ghost and was scared. Mr. Johnson found it hard to work, the day was long, and because it was winter that meant it would be dark again on the other side of his working day. All the way walking back home, Mr. Johnson could not stop himself from looking over his shoulder. And just before he got to his house a cold chill ran through his body, the exact same feeling as before when he had turned around to find he was all alone. He hurried on and when he got home he could see lights on in every room of his house. People were milling around on his front porch, making low whispered sounds. His wife was nowhere in sight. Where was Samuel, his little boy? Reverend Smith touched Mr. Johnson on the shoulder. Samuel has been hit by a wagon.

And your baby boy is dead.

My mother would end singing the phrase: Oh my Lord. Oh my Lord what shall I do?

Mother, do you think that that was the sound of a real ghost horse? I'm not sure but that's the way they told me the story. They say you can go to the cemetery in Auburn and see where little Samuel Johnson is buried. My mother said.

Long before my brother Winthrop died she had almost lost a child. She told us about Shurley, her first born, almost dying from pneumonia (which killed lots of people back then). A time when the doctor, grandmother, mother and everyone had done all they could with mustard plaster poultice to draw the phlegm and congestion out of his little chest. With four drops of kerosene dissolving a teaspoon of sugar to soothe his throat. Plus whatever syrups and pills the doctor carried with him house-to-house keeping sick people alive. Shurley was tiny when he had pneumonia, smaller than I am when she tells us. My mother sat waiting in the dark night warding off death all through the crisis, listening to baby small Shurley breathe his death-like rattle. Glad she could hear his breath. Everyone gathered to get him through the crisis. With mother guarding, the "crisis" passed over, Shurley got all better right after that.

I used to take out Mother and Daddy's album and look at the professional sepia photograph of Shurley as this incredible, dark-skinned beautiful, fat, perfectly healthy, round-faced baby sitting on a velvet draped stand. Now, here he sits beside me, being my brilliant knows-everything big brother, because the crisis passed.

Tish says, I am 63. I have already sung Happy Birthday to her, off key. I ask, how can that be? I usually keep you seven years old in my mind so we still can play school after school every day. My sister is all that is left of my growing up family. My daughter Tisha is her namesake, both reaching back to be named for my father's mother, Letitia.

Through the phone line my voice asks: Tish, do you remember coming back from The Alcazar when it was sort of dusk and then, after we had come up the hill and we were on Renwick, Shurley would kneel down and let me get on his back and then he would steady me into place and then you climbed on my shoulders?

Do you remember that?

Yes, and how could that be, after all he was no bigger than a minute. None of us were. What must we have looked like? Walking along after dark. Heading home. Like acrobats, I felt like we were acrobats. That is the way I can see all of us, Shurley and me and little round Tish on top. And Shurley not puffing or staggering, not once, under our weight. We would walk all the way down the block, get to the front porch steps, and then Shurley knew how to reach back and hold me while he lifted Tish down; then I climbed off in just a hop. Gentle and easy and expert.

Yeah, and what would any mother have thought? I hear Tish's laughter and query over the phone. Terrified, they'd scream:

Those children could fall and crack their heads open! You could get a hernia and be doubled over for the rest of your life! Any mother would say, Stop that's dangerous. Don't do that.

Don't-be-foolish, our mother would say.

She knew everything, could see through walls, around corners. She used to say, I've got eyes in the back of my head. Yes, and I believed her. But I don't think any one ever saw us. Maybe no one ever was there to witness the Harris Kids' Death Defying High Wire Act, on the sidewalk, balancing carefully. Alone on Renwick Avenue, after seeing Charlie Chan or The Lone Ranger or Our Gang. Hearing, above the sound of pounding hoof beat, Tonto yell, COME KEMOSABE!

The neighborhood movie was only a couple of blocks away. The Alcazar was one of the places we could go to all by ourselves. Almost every Saturday, after we had finished our weekly chores, when mother and Aunt Belle had come home from shopping. After lunch Winthrop and Shurley would take us to a matinee. It was the time of Shirley Temple, Jane Withers, Our Gang, Boston Blackie, the Bowery Boys and adventure serials. For ten cents we saw a sixty-minute feature, a cartoon, newsreel, and what the Lone Ranger did next to the bad guys. No matter how dark the cave or dastardly the trick, the Lone Ranger would escape in time to rescue the entire mining town. Sixty kids would rise in standing ovation with whistles and stomps to cheer his ingenuity. But before the end of the chapter, something else transpired that needed our shouted urgent instructions: Look out behind you. She's locked in the silo. Don't trust that guy.

THE LONE RANGER AND SILVER Chapter 47. To be continued....

We held our breath all week long. But my brothers and I knew that in spite of the marquee listing and his subservient-sounding Yes-Kemosabe, the Lone Ranger's Indian companion was the real savior. Not much good was going to happen on the screen without Tonto's wit, skill and strength. Jay Silverheels was a real Indian not some white guy with greasy makeup smeared on.

II

Why do I remember the glow of our living room lamp as yellow?

Nowadays lights are white or pale blue. That lamp in our square picture window was on every night whether anyone was in the living room or not. We turned it on to signify evening. We left it on in the empty house to welcome us any night the whole family, Mother, Daddy, Shurley, Winthrop, me and Tish, had all walked to Alcazar Movie Theater around the corner and down Castle. It was on when we came back from visiting Aunt Belle and Uncle Lawrencey so late that maybe one of us was carried in asleep.

A three bedroom, light-gray-with-white trim snug clapboard house. There was a wooden swing suspended in its frame stretched the exact length of the picture window, wide enough for Dolores and Adrian Lynch, me and Winthrop to squeeze safely after dark repeating ghost stories on the front porch until bedtime. The Lynches, they lived next door upstairs in a two-family house, with landlords

Mr. and Mrs. Williams on the first floor. All us kids would talk secretly across the Williams' driveway from second floor windows when we were supposed to be inside for homework or for sleep.

Our house had an attic that was playroom and storeroom. Not a real attic because there was no third floor, I suppose technically it was an unfinished fourth bedroom but we always called it attic and never questioned that it was on the second floor right next to the boys' room. The exposed beams inspired my big brother, Shurley, to cut rope and an old leather bag into an indoor swing. In the attic there was a corner where we could have real tea parties inside a big cardboard playhouse my Daddy had painted flower boxes and rose bushes on. Even though the attic was not a huge room, we were allowed to roller skate on rainy days. We raced laps.

My two older brothers had a silver metal dirigible (with small red wheels) that a family friend had given on a visit that wasn't even Christmas or birthday (I got a boring long-legged blonde doll that was sort of scary because she was almost as tall as I was). We could straddle this zeppelin and zoom across the floor. We were the only kids in the whole wide world with a ride-on toy like that. No one else had a swing inside their house. And the small attic window on the backyard wall was perfect for being Rapunzel on days that I could not go out to play, but my friend Dolores could and, as Prince, would call lovingly as I lowered my hemp rope hair to be rescued.

Croton School class picture

    My friends would come breathlessly to our back door each afternoon.
    Mrs. Harris, can Joan come out to play? House, dolls, jump rope, Statues, Russia, Kick the Can and hopscotch. Elaborate after-school games; like playing school, store, fire engine with real hose and real (step) ladder, or mud-pie bakery with cash register, hand-lettered receipts and wooden shelves, the kind of play that lasted every day for days or for weeks, planned drama, was set up at my house.

Except for Dolores and me, the kids were not colored. There were so few colored people in our whole neighborhood that from kindergarten to sixth grade all the other kids in my class were always white. In the whole school there was Johnny Hicks, Dolores and her two brothers, Adrian and Fitzhugh, and me, my older brothers, Shurley and Winthrop, and my little sister Letitia, whom we called Tish.

Although I was small for my age, it rarely mattered. If I had to hit a child, new to Croton School, for calling me nigger, I was tiny, but I was strong. And all of the other kids in my class knew the new kid was just plain wrong, they cheered me on. I'd be in trouble with the principal and my parents for fighting, but this new kid immediately understood his place did not sort out according to race. Sometimes by the time the new kid became an old ordinary kid, we might even be school friends.

Me, Joan Crawford, Dolores, and Marilyn would invent a school room, haul all the big things into the backyard, take turns being teacher, create lots of school supplies and spelling tests, erase the board, and clap erasers. My mother had bought a huge framed slate that she found at a rummage shop and my father built an easel support for it to stand on. We had a kid-size desk and play table and chairs, that would be added to cartons turned upside down so there could be rows of classroom seats. A long wooden pointer was essential for focusing attention, and for tapping on children's shoulders or drumming rhythmically on the floor. Mother kept us supplied with chalk. If there wasn't any chalk we would test which broken pieces of red brick wrote darkest, clearest, brightest on the sidewalk. Then we would fill the cement square with the times tables and rows of division go-zin-to's.

The competition was keen as we took turns playing the teacher. Preparing for play was often the noisiest energy, it was `brainstorming' but that was of course not our word. Children do it, they don't bother to name it, one idea would be cheered and added to another idea. The first Let's play school! would burst into choosing roles and gathering stuff. Books and pads, erasers and rulers. We might spend a day making a whole set of text books; cutting pages all the right size, illustrations drawn and colored with crayon, stiff book covers made from the backs of pads, decorated with pasted-on shiny flowers cut from mother's magazines, then sewed together with a big eye, blunt point children's needle. Flash cards cut to a precise size, miniatured because this was ours, and it was play. We would carefully match the lettering, put answers on the back so we could pretend to turn them over to check accuracy. (We made them; of course we knew the answers.) Then the flash cards would need a storage spot, which meant finding a box the right size, and shelves (boards stretched between stacked bricks) with a hand-lettered sign that said ARITHMETIC SUPPLIES. Drag out all of our own books plus those from the library, match them for a real reading lesson where all followed along in their own text.

And when the children had worked quietly and been obedient the teacher would announce a break to play a game, perhaps Eraser Race! The teacher could choose two students to come to the front of the classroom, stand back to back, balance a blackboard eraser on their head then circle the classroom as fast as they could run/walk while all the rest of the kids screamed and cheered their favorite. Some play teachers would dole out syrupy compliments and encouragement for the best work, and loud scolding for rude or lazy behavior. Everyone wanted first turn as teacher, because toward the end of play, more kids could get away with being rowdy students since you already had had your turn being teacher in charge. Our games lasted for hours, with carry-over to the next day or days when we were inventing some drama-elaborate. We would whisper and pass secret notes inside Croton School daydreaming about after-school play.

A new teacher came to Croton. She questioned me about my family; she insisted that I meant Flagstaff not Falstaff. I thought that seemed stupid, named after a city for no reason at all. Even when I said no, not Flagstaff, my grandmother taught high school English, she either did not believe me or just did not know Shakespeare well. So from the beginning I don't think that I liked her. One day she made me stay after school, declaring in front of my class that knew me, my book report was suspect. As I answered with questioned details, she acted disappointed. When I won a class spelling bee, her expression was surprise. Finally this strange young white woman started treating me like a pet. She let me clap the blackboard erasers two days in a row. I got to pass workbook papers out to the whole class. She started calling me her Little Chocolate Drop. I told my mother what she said. Mother sent a note to the principal to set up a conference.

When the school nurse marched into the room, our teacher sharply clapped her hands so class would line up for inspection. The school nurse could stalk into any classroom any time, she could interrupt anything. Even a test. Our teacher would signal for us to stand quickly and quietly beside our chairs, march to the front of the room aisle by aisle. Then form a long line that wound around the back by the storage shelves. No whispers, no giggles, take out your little key, lock your lips and throw the key away. We would march slowly by with our hands held out for Nurse Smith to inspect. Palms up, flip over. Scrubbed hands. Clipped fingernails. But she was really there to make sure there were no head lice. Lice could hop through the whole class. Nurse Smith carried a cardboard box filled with sticks slightly thicker than a toothpick but ten inches long. Using a new stick for each child so one head could not contaminate the next, she would snap the stick in half, then probe and lift your hair for signs of a single louse or louse egg.

It was the sound those slender sticks made as she clicked them, snap in two. It was the way she held them pinched at the very tip end as if direct contact with the child's head would make her rush to the bathroom, to throw up or to scour her hands with soapy hot water. Maybe she would have to do both.

The used pieces of stick were dropped to rattle ominously in the teacher's metal waste basket that had been placed at Nurse Smith's side. Each guilty kid was pulled by the arm to stand aside waiting until every child was examined; the rest of us were allowed to return to our seats.

We never seemed poor, we never looked poor, even at times we had no money. The white welfare kids were usually the ones who got sent home. At school, the people to be pitied or shunned were the poor white, grey-skinned children with thin sad straight hair chopped off to hang lifeless, bobbed just above their ear lobes.

I was the only one who never had to pray or worry about being embarrassed. I was the only one who was colored, and my kinky colored people's hair made me arrogant. Sometimes even clean rich white kids were caught and sent home with a note about treatment and exclusion until they could pass the nurse's hair examination. Head lice was much worse than a red Quarantine Sign tacked to your house's front door for scarlet fever or measles, worse even than being sent home with a note about ringworm.

Jenny Anderson's dull straight hair had cooties on almost every inspection. Jenny was white, dirt poor, and she always spelled easy words wrong, so only sometimes did we let her be friends on the schoolyard. In a bunch of us girls, seated cross-legged Indian style and together, someone asked blonde Betty Glazer, Is your hair naturally curly? It was. And the once in awhile when she wore Shirley Temple corkscrew curls, it did not need to be sectioned and tied in white strips of cloth overnight. Her hair simply had to be wet and curved around her mother's finger. How lucky! Then Jenny Anderson asked me, Joanie, is your hair naturally braided? The whole group of us really smart, sophisticated, second-grade girls snickered right in Jenny's bewildered face. (I sometimes wondered, but not out loud, if Jenny could have been smarter if she had been clean and better dressed.)

Norma Cohen and I were in-school friends and sometimes declared ourselves twins on our shared birthday, March 4, 1929. We both were good at spelling and arithmetic, with gold star papers tacked to the bulletin board. We both had dark hair. Norma's an above-the-ear-short bob, with the whole middle center pulled high into a cute top knot that stuck straight up, until the very tip end bent over to move briskly above the soft knot of a wide silk bowed ribbon, just like I wore. We were both very short. Norma was Jewish. I had dimples. Norma's mom gave an in-school birthday party with ice cream, cake, a store-bought Pin-The-Tail-On-The-Donkey, plus favors for the entire second grade. Norma and I both wore black velveteen dresses with hand-crocheted collars to the party, and my mom sent cupcakes for the teacher and the whole class.

Lots of kids in my class took after-school lessons at their Catholic Church and then got to make communion, dressed in white. Boys in crisp white short-pants suits. My friend Joy Kambas and all of the Catholic girls who were ready wore bridal gowns! I wanted a bride's dress. A short white lace dress, white gloves, white stockings, white mary janes, a small Bible with hanging white ribbon bookmark that had a sharp inverted v cut out at each end. And a true bride's veil attached to pink rose buds held in place on your head with three small white side combs. I taught Joy pig Latin. Joy taught me how to say her name in Greek, Zoiii Kahmbachulaki. We were learning to write cursive and long division. Joy was my age. How could a seven-year-old get married? To whom?

In our African Methodist Episcopal Zion Church we did not make communion, we took it. The first Sunday of every month, lining up to solemnly walk to the front of the church and eat broken matzo, Jewish cracker, and drink just a sip of sweet sweet dark purple grape juice from tiny tiny glasses the deacons held arranged squeezed in tight circles on round silver trays. Every first Sunday I wanted desperately to keep my tiny emptied crystal glass in the palm of my hand and take it home so I could use it when I played house with my dolls. I was not sure how to steal, I knew that one did not do it and I was positive that stealing in His House guaranteed immediate bolt of lightning. My mother would be mortified. But there were so many, jammed on each of several trays, they were the perfect size for my doll Mary's mouth, and the grape juice, strangely sweeter than sugar and molasses mixed in honey, instead tasted bitter. My jaws clenched and trembled as I swallowed what was (I thought) real wine. It was hard to concentrate on why I had walked down to the crowded chancel. I only knew I was surrounded.

All Catholics got to show off that they were praying. Each time Catholics prayed In The Name Of The Father (even silently) they made a sign advertising Jesus' crucifix. I knew it was my Jesus too, but no one would have wanted me to cross over the rules. I practiced secretly, in the attic, blessing my own forehead, shoulders and heart. Praying that I got the right order, in case it counted which part of my body I touched first.

III

My father hated being poor. Hated the struggle to meet bills whenever business was slow. My mother was the one who redefined poverty. She dragged him through lessons on how you made make-do seem better. We could not convince my father of the adventure part. My mother stretched dimes and pennies back when dimes and pennies bought a complete meal for a family. But my father hated knowing how. How expert she was at keeping us going just reminded him of being without money. He hated kerosene lamps, stubs of candles and macaroni and cheese bought out of necessity. He couldn't laugh about our friendly old ragman.

The rag man was small, gray, Jewish. His accent was mid-European and his beard, kinky. He and his horse seemed both very old. On a day we were completely without money, even for food, I was posted as look-out. The sound of horse hooves meant either the ragman or huckster at this time of day, because the milkman's wagon was heard so early in the morning that it was still dark outside. The milkman's sound was tip-toe quiet. His horse moved slow and too muffled to actually wake anyone up, but if I was awake tucked safe under my blankets it was a nice noise, the horse would blow breath and the milkman sometimes answered low sweet to him. In chorus the clean empty returned bottles' clink-rattled like milkman music within the sides of the divided metal carrier the milkman toted as he walked from our porch back to his horse and wagon.

On a day we needed to sell rags I'd sit on the bottom porch step to hear the ragman as soon as I could. Raaaaaags? Any old rags today. Any old rags? rang up the street half-a-block before I could see him. I would run to the curb to stop him, then dash into the house and get mother. My brothers, and even baby Tish, my mother and I had been digging and throwing all morning to fill the burlap bags that he'd left from the last time. By the time the horse lopped down the street to our house the wagon was already piled high. It took forever for the ragman to pull, lift, poke and rearrange the stack so that a new bag of rags could be added. His thick Yiddish accent was so wet and folded, sometimes I could not understand what he said, but mother always did; she had learned a few phrases in his language from the neighborhood where we lived when I was a baby. Mother would throw in a few words from her high school German, and I would look up at the two of them as they soared to another country talking, smiling. Laughing at jokes? Familiar as two old friends, they would begin negotiating in English/German/Yiddish. They bargained back and forth as if they were related then settled on a per-pound price as he hoisted the hand-held scales to sunlight. Mother checked and corrected the pointer reading at least twice every time the ragman visited, then they exchanged goods for money. They promised, See you next week Mrs. Harris. Wednesday, Mr. Fein?

Mother made a grocery list and sent me across the street to the store. I think Shurley was embarrassed to count out coins to Mr. Johnson right after the ragman had been seen on our block. I was smart-alecky proud of counting skill and bargaining as I measured out nickels and dimes for ingredients for the night's casserole and something to drink. Flavorade, two packs for a penny or milk at ten cents a quart, depending on how much change was left.

We always had clothes that could be sold as rags to buy dinner. We only had to search quickly and carefully. There were things in the drawstring bag of cleaning rags or collected fabric in the rag bundle of saved articles for mother's crocheted rugs that she sold or made for our house. And there was always a dress, sweater or jacket that was not wanted or did not fit. From the secondhand store, to mother, to the ragman, to mother, to Mr. Johnson the storekeeper, to mother, to us.

Daddy's creativity all went into his art; he wasn't very good at making-do. But, on Sunday he made breakfast. Late in the morning, still in pajamas, we'd already have finished reading Alley Oop, Katzenjammer Kids and Orphan Annie, stretched flat on our stomachs all over the living room floor, vaguely listening to rumbling, banging sounds from the kitchen. Mother sat, keeping him company, at the kitchen table. This was his show. One egg on request, fried over, up or scrambled? Even poached, in a specific toy-sized pan, if you wanted a wet egg. Bacon thick-sliced from a slab, two pieces for Daddy, one and a half for mother and Shurley and one slice each for the rest of us. With chef's flair Daddy presented the pièce-de-résistance, after everyone was seated, one small can of grapefruit that he stretched by adding water. The reduced juice reached almost the brim of our saucer and the diluted liquid washed away all flavor from the three lonesome grapefruit sections we each had. Taking Mother's cue, our enthusiastic thank-you's gave him E for effort.

Daddy's work at the studio ranged from small still life to mural, to commercial advertising, portraits with sittings in his studio or a client presenting a photograph to be rendered in oils. I didn't know that real art was supposed to be better than sign painting. I preferred signs. Huge block letters, marked out on gigantic swaths of oilcloth, were wonder. Signs were quick and bright.

His oil paintings were slow moving, flat and muddy. It took much too long to stand and watch, besides I would not be allowed to touch the portrait in progress. He let me help lay out the penciled outline for a paper sign. I could actually do part of the hand-cut silk-screen stencil, for a sign repeated on card stock. At a time when I was just beginning to master staying inside the lines of my coloring book, I saw my father paint broad free strokes bold with careless speed. It was magic that had more to do with this magician than just being an adult. The other kids' fathers did not do this work; the other kids' fathers did not let them help produce their work. The other kids, most of them, hardly knew what their fathers did for work, they only knew they went to it. My daddy sometimes took me with him, and we worked together.

He did commercial art for businesses like Bresee Auto, Rexall Drug, or Henry Jackson's small dry cleaning store. Sometimes I could help with huge advertisements laid out on gigantic rolls of oil cloth or white butcher paper. I learned measuring, ratio, perpendicular, parallel, proportion, perspective and movement of angles as my father taught me to sketch and do layout on his quick small pad and transformed the bare idea to bright come-on that filled an automobile dealership window. Even the full-page *Post Standard* illustration that I would see weeks later, when my brother's friend Roy delivered our paper, was my father's work.

After Daddy tried his ideas on a drawing pad, he did not need a yardstick as straight-edge, the way we used a ruler in school, tediously measuring line by inch. With his T-square plus a large chunk of blue chalk and length of string as compass to snap the guideline, he would lightly sketch the lettering as fast as a scribble, paint signs so big they did not fit on his massive work table. He would paint the first letters, the first words, and roll part of the sign up as it dried, and he moved on to the finish. And it all came out even; without checking back, it all matched, the lines continued straight and true because the first section was parallel. By swinging the string centered to a thumb tack compass you did not have to use the T-square over and over. Daddy ran his fat hunk of blue draftsman's chalk along the string, fastened one end down, pulled the chalk-colored string perfectly taut and snapped down a temporary marking to keep the tops and bottoms of each letter amazingly straight. On some days I would be the one to pull the tight blue dusted string onto Mr. Bresee's sign. And it worked even when I did it, with my father's help. I knew the language of my father's work and could tell other kids. I felt comfortably smart. Special. I was surrounded by a teaching family.

When I was four or five my father showed me how an artist sees. Just lie back and gaze up at the ceiling without remembering that the room is a cube. Just look at the corners on the ceiling and see how they are shaped, examine the angles as obtuse rather than right. A lot of time we would lie on the bed laughing at Charlie McCarthy and Edgar Bergen, Fibber McGee and Molly, but our favorite show was Information Please, because the questions were really hard and the experts on the panel were very, very smart.

I would stare at the ceiling's corner, move across to the next, circle the four, then back again, and then again. He treated me as if I were an adult. And because he spoke to me of perspective and composition, form follows function, obtuse and acute, when I was only three or four, I went to school at five and astounded the teachers with vocabulary and with reasoning. And the spotlight was often on me. At home all that was accepted and expected. All of us Harris kids were smart.

My father was a sometimes gentle teacher, and his formal classroom was the studio. It felt gigantic. Open, yet filled and busy all at the same time. Daddy's studio smelled different than the rooms of my house; the glue and turpentine, the woods, oil, chalk, treated canvas and heat. And the tools. My father loved expensive, finely designed tools and materials. He would open a case at a beginning work session, lift, then name each article with reverence. I memorized their names. I thought the containers alone were beautiful. How they were put together could be an ingenuous surprise. The doeskin, soft leather envelope with inside and outside pouches closed folded over to fasten with long leather ribbon ties; two worn miniature cowhide trunks; a mahogany box with thin shelves and nesting boxes for pen nibs and holders. There was a large rough pine box with handle and hinges of burnished brass that popped up shelves and compartments holding charcoal, chalk, and thick flat wood pencils, and small tubes of oil paint.

It was easy to fall in love with all of those magical belongings. My father taught me to respect and value the design of good and useful tools. I know the feel of an expensive camel-hair paint brush. A vast difference from those he had of boar. My father let me see what the better brush could do. How a single brush handled by skilled fingers could produce infinite width, texture and shading as he twirled, stabbed and spun the smooth maple wood handle. There were brushes with handles as slender as a toothpick and others an inch in diameter. Daddy would sweep the soft bristles across my cheek. I held my hand properly palm up to feel how gentle the brush must swish across the canvas for one effect, more boldly press and flow for a different coloring.

Father's studio was his classroom but the whole house was where my mother taught, and the rules less restrictive; no one ever cautioned: Quiet, your mother is cooking. Daddy did not say, stay out of the dining room your mother is working. Don't disturb your mother, she's dusting now. No one said, Did you ask your mother if you could use her broom? In fact all tools for cleaning held generic possession (the broom, the mop, the dustpan), though the job of keeping the house clean was her work. There was no particular space that was my mother's room only.

There was always the sound of poetry and singing when my mother worked alongside of us kids. Her repertoire encyclopaedic, sometimes as embracing background to our chores, sometimes entertainment as a one-woman show. Sometimes I would hear her softly singing only to herself when I was all the way upstairs in bedroom or attic.

Once in awhile, if I was home from school, sort of sick, I'd spread blankets and pillow on the attic floor to read and through the open window I could hear Mr. Manley, the gym teacher, give his commanding clap that kept proper rhythm for the marching on the playground. My house at the top of the hill, playground below, I would listen to my school's sound float in and wish I was there for outdoor gym class' circled marching, dodge ball and jumping jacks in place. I would close my eyes and practice catching enough air in my cupped palms wishing that I knew how to send crisp sharp sound a whole block away.

My school friends and neighborhood friends were mostly the same kids. By the time I entered school I was following Shurley and Winthrop. Teachers referred to me as their little sister, and several of my friends were little sisters to some of my big brothers' friends. My friend Joan was the little sister of Shurley's friend, Roy Crawford.

Me, Joan, and Marilyn Cox had been speeding our tall tricycles all afternoon. We were cops! Bent across the handlebars zooming back and forth in front of my house (I could ride out of sight down the hill only with special permission). Joan claimed that she was going to get a two-wheel bicycle in the summer, right after school let out. Nunnh unh, I didn't believe her. Her brother Roy had a bike but he was a teenager. Young school kids with wheels had wagons, scooters, clamp-to-your-shoe roller skates and large tricycles. We never even sat on a bike. Marilyn's brother's old bike was in the shed behind her house. We decided to go to only just look at it.

Inside it was sort of dark, the rusted old bike with not even both wheels was wedged half way under a pile of junk. If I had any idea of how to hold it up and start pedaling, there would be no way to ride it up the hill. But I could drag it home to my backyard, and my brother Shurley'd be sure to figure some way to fix it. And paint it. And put one gold lightning bolt on each side of the front wheel fender.

What Are You Doing In There?

Screaming out of nowhere, Mrs. Cox scared us half to death. I caught my breath and let Marilyn explain exactly when she had come back home without coming straight in the house to let her mother know she was home. Then we had to lie about whether I had my mother's permission to come down the street and cross a street because Mrs. Cox'd gotten so mad and even if we did scare her, she scared us and didn't even say she was sorry. I still wanted that piece of old bike, it probably wasn't the best time to talk about it but Mrs. Cox had screamed and asked a straight-out question so of course we answered exactly what we were doing. Plus I was thinking we were not sneaking around in the dark. We were looking and it happened to be dark in there. Marilyn did all of the talking I only nodded my head in the lie about my mother's permission.

She said, I don't think so.

She said, The bike is broken.

Mrs. Cox said, Tell your mother I will sell it to you for $5.

So I ran up the hill and into the house with my breathless proposition and could hardly hear my mother saying that I'd again left my tricycle in the middle of the sidewalk where someone could trip or fall. And kill themselves. In the middle of: Mother, Isn't-five-dollars-a-bargain? Isn't-it? I swore to always pull my trike to the backyard and out of the way the next time (forever next times).
    And mother said, No!
    She said, Don't be foolish!
    She said, Absolutely not!
    $5 for broken trash? My mother asked.

    A really good friend's mother would have said you can have that old bike if you think that your big brother can fix it up. And Shurley would have fixed it. Shurley could have made it brand new, transformed those rusted pieces, painted a lightning bolt on each side of the front fender. And it would have been my whatever-color-I-wanted bike with me whizzing off. Down the hill. And all the way around the block.

IV

  I remember growing up in Syracuse, New York in the 1930s as pleasant. That is so strange, how could that be? My father could not always make enough money to support us, some of the time we were on Soldiers and Sailors Relief. The fact that absolutely everybody-else-in-the-world was also poor, softens the edge. It was the Depression; a whole lot of people were in the same place. For my mother it seemed that being without was a way to create adventurous possibilities. Seems like we must have been struggling, but most of the time we didn't look like we were suffering.

  She let us play. My mother did not exactly play with us; still she played into our imaginations and games. A walk was not a walk, I could be a hobo traveling across the world with my lunch gathered in a red bandana tied to a stick. She would help us pack lunch. Do you want a bean sandwich? My mother made and ate baked beans spread between two pieces of wheat bread. With a little mayonnaise. Lots of times. She liked them. This was the woman who loved liver and onions or Limburger cheese or pickled pigs' feet. My mother relished calves' brains!

But she was only kidding when she reached toward the kettle of navy beans warming on the back of the stove. Our sandwiches would be bologna and mustard. Winthrop cooked the thick bologna slices in the cast-iron fry pan, letting it puff like a dome in the middle, brown around the edge. Flip it over with a spatula before it burned black. Or maybe our sandwiches would be home-ground-peanuts, peanut butter spread on saltine, wrapped in waxed paper and popped into a brown paper bag. We would take a Boy Scout canteen of Flavorade or water and our collapsible aluminum cups.

With repeated cautionary instruction, Stay-together, Look-both-ways, Don't eat your sandwiches up first thing, my brother and I were off on safari that could last as long as we wanted. Armed with a mason jar for bugs, we saw or captured all sorts of wild things: two-inch-long green grasshoppers that spit tobacco juice on your hand trying to scare you into thinking it was poison so you would drop them and they could get away; tiny brown baby grasshoppers that had not learned how to spit; smooth bright lucky stones; true daisies and small weed-flower daisies with thread-thin petals; transparent-winged cicada beetles; thick-stemmed milkweed plant with its curious sticky white sap that gave the plant its name. The milkweed had pods shaped like a small green bird and when you eased the pod apart there were silk damp white strings clustered into an oval pack. It always felt like we'd been away for hours and hours, probably walked a hundred miles, because my mother let us make the time and space determination. How did she know?

Some days we were on search and mission, not simply fantasy hike. We took a cloth bag to fill up with pounds of dandelion leaves, and Shurley's jack-knife to cut away the stem and blossoms. Once back home and in our kitchen the greens were rinsed, culled, and cut, to be boiled down, flavored with smoked neck bones or pigs knuckles, one of the best early spring dinners. Probably we were gone an hour, maybe half.

I was in kindergarten, so Winthrop was just nine years old. Our trusted independence had this simple rule: Go as far as you like as long as you follow the path of the railroad tracks, then turn around. The tracks will bring you right back home. I felt smug and amazed that this worked every time. My mother was so smart. We walked until we could not see our house, not see Mr. Johnson's store sign, the maple tree or anything else that was on our block. Were we in another town?

No, I guess not. But we had gone far away.

Most of the time, we led a life of staying safe at home; in the attic playroom, the back yard, on the porch, or on the sidewalk as far as the next house in either direction. There was a grocery store right on the corner near our house and there was another one around the other corner and down the block. Mr. Johnson's was the one across the street. Mrs. Arkin, sweet short old woman, with a European Jewish accent and store half the size of Mr. Johnson's, was across the street from Croton Elementary School. She carried candy, hard salami, hard rolls, halvah, ice cream push-ups, Eskimo Pies, milk, Flavorade and fat kosher pickles. When you stepped into her store it was so tiny you were immediately at the counter. There was a pay phone high on the wall in back on the customer side, very narrow space for the person on the phone, especially after school or at noon when kids piled in to buy treats.

On very hot summer days, so hot that even kids were bored and limp, we would watch and wait to see if Mr. Johnson would bring an old wooden chair to sit outside the store door and fan himself. Why did we think he had a way of knowing the weather? It didn't matter how many times he was right or the fact that his predictions were either obvious or fairly vague, Mr. Johnson was our source, so that we could begin to plan, to get ready, to put on bathing suits, and run outside in the rain. When I grew impatient waiting for him to appear I would post myself with both feet balanced on the base of the street light, grab hold with my left hand, sway my body out at seventy-degree angle spinning around and around to throw my voice across the road as loud as I could, Mr. Johnson. Mr. Johnson. Mr. Johnson. Mr. Jaaaahhhn...son, is it going to rain today?" He always answered. The reason we thought he was the weatherman was because he never said I don't know and once in a while, often enough, he was right. He would come out of the store, look up at the sky that I could have looked at, study the clouds or check the clear blue and give his personal prediction: not today. It's too bright today. We might get a shower in the afternoon. We would sing Thank you, Mr.Johnson. With perfectly serious smile he would go back to his work with canned goods.

When clouds showed obviously imminent rain, I could trust enough to go inside and badger my mother to let me put my swimsuit on now, because Mr. Johnson said it is going to rain and that way I'll be all ready. On any of those perfect days, Winthrop, me and Dolores would sit on the steps in bright colored wool jersey knit swimsuits and rubber bathing caps with tight chin straps anticipating the summer shower. Ready to leap out under the very first drop as soon as it fell. Dressed in swimsuits we could splash in the deepest, muddiest puddles, the kind that were off-limits walking home in boots and school clothes.

So whose game was this anyway? My mother's? Mr. Johnson's? Mine and hers? Or was it more of Mother's subtle teaching that more than half the joy is in the planning?

I can feel the vertical ridges of the lamppost column inside the palm of my hand. Today, simply by concentrating, I am back to the corner of Renwick and Raynor, twirling, trusting scarecrow-thin Mr. Johnson, in his white canvas apron, forecaster for rainy weather.

I wasn't allowed to go to either Mr. Johnson's or Mrs. Arkin's without permission. But at five I was old enough for errands, and I went with a penny for candy and a list for food. You could see Mr. Johnson's store from our front porch. We went there most, it was so close, had real groceries, and he kept a small spiral topped note pad with Mr. and Mrs. Harris written across the top of one page. Sometimes we would go to Mr. Johnson, read our list and then say, Can you trust us 'till Friday? Mr. Johnson would write each item and cost on our page in his book, say sure and he would.

My mother would call me from playing to run across the street to the store. Put the money in your handkerchief. Let me see, is the corner tied tight?

She read aloud as she named each item that she wrote. A loaf of wheat bread. Five cents worth of macaroni. A ten-cent piece of cheese. And a bag of salt. Then I would have to recite back to her exactly what she had said, A loaf of wheat bread, five cents worth of macaroni, a ten-cent piece of cheese and a bag of salt. It was important for me to know what I was shopping for and essential to start with, Good-Morning-Mr. Johnson, and to remember please and thank you as part of the list. My mother watched me cross the street even though I had learned how to look both ways (and the intersection was about as busy as a country lane).

The building on the corner looked like a neat, small clapboard house except the whole front downstairs was a plate glass window with his arch-shaped painted store name, JOHNSON'S

GROCERY. The store-plus-storage-room took up most of the first floor. And instead of lawn or front yard there was solid sidewalk to the curb. Mr. Johnson lived in the back, with part of his living rooms upstairs behind the white ruffled cotton curtains framing two windows that faced the street. An open bell with a clapper let him know there was a customer when I came through the door. He would come out, lean on the counter, and wait for me to shop from my list, checking casually when I had finished to see if there was anything I had forgotten to 'read' to him. While he measured from the wheel of sharp cheddar cheese I started the preliminary examination of the huge glass counter of penny candies. It would take me a very long careful time to make the right decision. I had lots of favorites. On top of the counter Mr. Johnson had rows of Grab Bags lined up on a white enamel tray if you wanted to be surprised. Inside each small, folded tightly, brown paper bag you could get a jumbled mix for two cents. Just like leftovers. But it was always a gamble that the bag could be filled with stuff that you mostly did not like. The days I found maybe three spearmint leaves, one orange slice, two chocolate covered malted milk balls and a long black licorice whip were bliss. Every single time I chose candy I took... forever. Mr. Johnson waited easily.

Running an errand felt grown up, I was not usually allowed far from home. Even across the street was some place.

In our house there was a baby grand piano (my mother played), a floor model radio, two filled ebony bookcases, and a hand-crocheted, room size rag rug in the living room. My mother made that rug and some smaller ones in the other rooms. Dark tweed-like colors chosen carefully, looped intricately with a fat polished-wood crochet hook.

There was a maple tree in the front yard and a cigar tree at the side back porch. I should look up the real name of that tree. We named it cigar because the seeds were long narrow hanging brown bunches.

There were books in almost every room of our house. Our kids' books: The Bobbsey Twins, Tom Swift, Grimm Brothers, *American Indian Fairy Tales* pictured by John Rae and titled To Young America From The Oldest American, *Josie and Joe*. A set of *Books of Knowledge* and the piles of yellow *National Geographic* magazines. No one else had books in the way or space that we did. When did I pay attention to that difference? The bottom shelves of the living room bookcases were filled with a set of dusky-green linen-bound encyclopedia with spines as broad as the length of my hand. Almost everything you wanted to know was in our encyclopedia. Shurley gave informal lectures on anything: science, geography, art. When the toads he brought back from a hike had a marking that was different from toads already in his personal back-porch swampland, he found where to start his informational search in the fat green books.

Dunbar, Countee Cullen, Phillis Wheatley, W.E.B. Du Bois' *The Souls of Black Folk* (back when we were all colored) plus his *Crisis* magazine that came to Daddy by mail. Art books often too tall, were stacked horizontally on shelves, or on the floor on Daddy's side of their bed. Photographs of sculpture, charcoal or pencil sketches, nudes, still life, landscape, portraits, Daddy's current pad he used to work through change of a developing project. His saved sketch pads from long-ago university assignments in still and life class, and newspaper articles in scrapbooks.

Back then there were two nationally distributed Negro newspapers and my father subscribed to both; the *Amsterdam News* out of New York City and the *Pittsburgh Courier*. What I can never forget is the reports of lynchings and of how afraid I stayed. There were so many, week after week after week. In the kitchen, Daddy would read to Mother, He was beaten to death.

Then hanged.

Dead or still alive what was left of this tortured Negro man, the white men and boys would douse with oil and set on fire. The next day, all the people, probably even children, would see his burned black body hanging from the tree where he'd been lynched.

I was scared that we, my daddy and my brother Shurley, could not be safe even though we lived way up north. Who had to cut him down the day after he was killed? Would they wrap him in a quilt? Who climbed the tree? What if the only person was the man's own little boy? Why didn't the rope burn? Would his skin crack and still hurt him after he was dead? That's one of the things I remember about the black newspapers, the lynchings that kept happening. White papers hardly printed a word.

When I was about nine or ten, there was a big newspaper story about Marian Anderson. (I did not like Marian Anderson.) The Daughters of the American Revolution would not let the famed contralto perform in Constitution Hall because she was a Negro. From all of Daddy's newspapers you could tell that the whole country was up in arms over the DAR's insult, and it felt like the fury went on for months. Colored people had been keeping up with all that DAR mess in the *Pittsburgh Courier* and the *Amsterdam News*. There were stories in the regular white papers and a whole lot in Daddy's *Daily Worker*. It was big news.

Well, I did not like Marian Anderson. That was not something to admit out loud. Of course I was worried. You were not supposed to not like Marian Anderson. I don't think it was allowed. The Daughters of the American Revolution publicly did not like Miss Anderson. Mrs. Eleanor Roosevelt stepped in to organize a huge concert. On Easter Sunday, April 9, 1939, Marian Anderson sang for 75,000 people gathered at the steps of the Lincoln Memorial in Washington, D.C.

Miss Anderson's hair lay in heat-crimped marcel waves, the same style as my mother wore. But Marian Anderson's singing did not sound like my mother singing. Miss Marian Anderson made even hymns sound like opera.

My mother hummed as background to dish washing, performed loud Irish ballads to move the carpet sweeper back and forth, sang verse and chorus to Sometimes I Feel Like A Motherless Child, as Tish and I sat under the dining room table polishing its carved legs. The reason I loved, still love, Paul Laurence's When Malindy Sings is because Mother could croon smooth Dunbar dialect as she recited, and it felt like he had written about my mother's voice.

> ... fu' real melojious music Dat jes' strikes yo' hea't and clings, Jes' you stan' an lissen wif me When Malindy sings.

When I was a little girl, one of my best heroes was Eleanor Roosevelt. Eleanor Roosevelt. Amelia Earheart, the aviatrix. And Mary McLeod Bethune. Mary McLeod Bethune started a college for colored ladies simply because it was something that should be done and so she did it. I was sure Mrs. Bethune and Mrs. Roosevelt were best friends, because I saw their pictures all the time in the *Pittsburgh Courier* as they sat whispering together at meetings or Ladies Afternoon Tea.

I was sorry I didn't like Marian Anderson, I'd go around with explanations inside my head. It certainly wasn't because she was dark-skinned. I had the biggest crush on Junior Clair because his skin was jet black. Not because she was homely, I adored Mary McLeod Bethune's bulldog-shaped face. But while everyone (including my own family) raved about her voice, I thought that it quavered low, off key and from some deep miserable place in her body. She clasped her hands at her stomach and pushed that voice past her tonsils, and out of a mouth formed into a small stiff O. Not only singing, even talking her voice bothered me, because I hated when she called herself, one instead of I. Inside I would cringe when she squeezed out that number. I wanted her to say me and I. Or mine! I think that they hurt her feelings really bad. But one did not lower oneself to rudeness.

 Back then, one was not raised to keen.

Young Falstaff and Evelyn

V

My father would proudly announce, I have dreamed every single night of my life. Even in muddy foxholes in France! He didn't then tell his dreams, just wanted to note that he was a man who always dreamed.

When I was little I would balance on the tips of my father's cordovan oxfords as he danced me across the floor. When I was little I would listen to my father fast plinking his mandolin, Mother humming in the background on the nights there was nothing on the radio worthwhile. I wish he had taught me to play that quick-stringed drum. I wish I had asked who taught him?

All my life, books and notebooks always stay tumbled on the floor beside my bed. That is like my father.

I like that.

Trying to remember my father: he is in bed. Not asleep, just in bed. Sometimes even in the daytime, head hung over mattress edge to closely examine some research or oversize color-filled art book.

His study is intense.

I don't remember my mother ever even lying down in the daytime. I used to brag, inside my head just to myself, my mother never took a nap. Never! Well, except she was lying on the floor once when I was small; I found her in the dining room beside the table. I remember I was too small to actually see what was on the table unless I climbed up on a chair. I yelled for help. Now, I wonder if maybe she was pregnant and had fainted.

She was lying on the couch, I was bigger then, beginning to be an adolescent. My father was kneeling on her chest and punching her in the face and I was screaming and scratching and pulling, pushing, grabbing him off. That was daytime, I can see us. We all have our daytime clothes on.

It was not exactly a secret my father drank and beat my mother, my brother Shurley and me. I always knew, without talking about it much at the time or later. It was not lost, just not remembered often. In my family my father twisted Mother's arms to the middle of her back. Shurley's arm to middle of his back. Pulled and twisted my arm high to the middle of my back. My father slapped, knocked down, kicked, and punched. And we fought back the best we could. If you are punched in the face hard enough you can really see sparks that flash in a spray. I remember, I watched, so this is what it means, hit so hard you see stars. There is also a sound.

We pounded his shoulders, his face, his back and screamed. We cried, gouged his flesh with our fingernails. And we ran. My mother would whisper, Get your coat. Put on your shoes. Then she held our hands tight in hers as she led our escape into the dark, away from beatings. I remember how she kept talking softly, telling nighttime stories about everything we passed. A dark version of daytime walks she took us on to discover a building being torn down with huge clanging iron ball or perhaps a crater being dug to lay foundation of stone for structure to rise. Perhaps we headed nowhere to pick wildflowers. Now we are in a midnight walk to a silenced construction site, past a walled-in junkyard's clutter. Through the slots of wooden plank fencing I peer transfixed by the sharp slanted rust jumble and the perfectly still steel tall-towering crane. We never talked about why we were in the street at this hour. We never said anything about creeping back home when he had fallen into safe, deep snoring.

If he had my mother pinned so that neither Shurley nor I, not even the two of us together, could pull him off, could pin back his flailing fists, she, her face would turn from underneath to plead a soft, call-the-police. I was the one to leave and search. Shurley was stronger, more able to maybe stay at least some of the blows. I was fast. I could run. And I hated having to let anyone know that my family, that my mother, that we needed policemen to save her life because I had not stopped him. No matter what I did. I hated begging for the call when I'd forgotten to bring a nickel with me. I hated the wasted time it took to calm my heart, my breath and voice. And tell.

I got back to my house before the police did. My mother had brushed down her hair, straightened her clothes, the dining room. My father sat finished in the living room chair.

Now, I could not imagine her dead.

The police (white men of course) not young, always brusque, came in pairs and filled my silent house.

Sympathetic to my now quiet father, accepting his business card, they spoke together and. they. left. him. It would not stop. Repeat. Repeat. Repeat. They would not take him away. I did not want my father arrested. She could not be dead. No one would let that happen? My mother would not leave me. Ever.

The morning after. My mother would begin to create secrets, between just her and us kids. She would go over the whole night's wrangle, picking only the bits that could be funny, putting us to work as straight man for her stand-up routine.

And how about trying to teach us his Bill Robinson dance lessons?

Then with no stage makeup to cover her cheek bruise, in pastel plaid cotton house dress Evelyn would execute an exquisite parody of drunken Falstaff's time step. (Taught impromptu, one Negro artist to another, backstage at Syracuse's big Keith's Theatre downtown. And my father's teacher was Bill Robinson, the real Bojangles!, the one we could see showing Shirley Temple how to dance on the Alcazar neighborhood movie screen. For ten cents a ticket.)

    Kalump 2 cross-over 4
    Clunk 2 stagger 4
    Hands on hips tip 2 hop one
    (then she sort of waggled her head)
    Tap ttt tap ttt tap tap tap tap
    Tap ttt tap ttt tap tap tap tap

    She was funny. Of course we knew what she was doing, beside the kitchen table that had been crashed over, pans clattering, dishes shattered, glass splinters flying sharp. Last night.
    The morning after We Howled!

    Sometimes my mother recited an extravagant Delsarte Declamation to make us laugh. Her swooping, heartrending performance of the Victorian elegy, The Face on the Bar Room Floor, verse after verse after verse of a little tike's mission to call her father back home from demon rum. One day, inspired by melodrama, my sister and I plotted our own dear father's transformation.
    To us redemption seemed a perfect possibility. We were both witness to the times that our father was gentle and loving. Why would anyone choose being drunk? We huddled on the toy chairs at the toy table inside the playhouse in the corner of the attic composing a storybook plea on lined paper, changing a poor word to a better one, sounding out phonetically correct spelling, printing neatly,

using up one sheet, two sheets and another sheet of paper as rubber erasing smudged too gray for this important missive. What did it say? I can't really remember: Daddy, please don't get drunk anymore? Stop hitting Mommy? Don't make me go call the police ever again? I do remember how we worked steady, heads together all afternoon. There were hugs and kisses, OOOO XXXX, because that is what Tish could draw/write all by herself. Then we folded it neatly, printed DADDY uppercase, propped it in full view on top of the pile of books on the floor beside our father's side of their bed.

We checked the next morning and the note was gone. My father and mother never mentioned it. We waited. And nothing changed. If at least he had said, I read your letter, then walked away. Said, Don't you girls ever do that again! Said, Daddy was only a little bit drunk. Said anything.

I could not stop it. I had enlisted Tish, and failed. In secret I wept, then declared a covenant: I Would Never Be Anything Like My Father, and the first separation: I Would Stop Reading Books.

I'd show him.

Except in school. Because in school I was adored and happy. My parents loved getting good reports so I kept up all the reading that Miss McManus assigned. Including book reports. And reading to Tish did not count as my reading. At home no one noticed my searingly dramatic change. Not my father. Or my mother. Not even Shurley and Winthrop.

No one! When I look back it feels like my grudge match went on for several years. Who knows about time, real time? Maybe my unsigned boycott lasted only a few months.

> Father dear father come home with me now
> The clock in the tower strikes ten....

I never knew it was a hangover. Now the house was calm. On Daddy's morning-after he would let me watch or sometimes actually open and prepare, the magical (pre-Alka-Seltzer) medicine called Seidlitz Powders. It came in two separate blue thin papers. You needed two tall drinking glasses. First, you half filled each glass with water, sprinkled one and then the other secret packet slowly. Then quickly poured the foaming potion back and forth back and forth back and forth from glass to glass carefully. No matter. Still it fizzles over the edge and makes me an amazed sorceress.

VI

All of my growing up life my Williams cousins lived in Syracuse. And my grandmother, Aunt Pauline (mother's older sister), Uncle Al, and the Morehand cousins lived together in Auburn, N.Y. not far away. My mother's mother had smooth-to-the-touch red brown skin, a quiet voice, was much shorter than five feet tall and she had bright white soft kinked hair (that she never straightened). All of our family stories say that my grandfather was a gentle disciplinarian who loved and judiciously spoiled his youngest daughters Isabel and (my mother) Evelyn who were often summoned and/or referred to with one blur name Isaba-evelyn. They were called twins as children and continued to be devoted to each other when they grew up to be my mother and aunt. I did not know Grandpa Diggs, he died when Shurley was still a baby, but he was real to me with all the when-I-was-a- kid stories my mother told in comedy or proverb. My grandmother still lived in the house that my mother grew up in on Fitch Avenue in Auburn that Dan Diggs had bought when he was earning $7 a week at the rope factory.

Only 28 miles from Syracuse, a weekend trip to Grandmother's was as delicious and noisy as a European Grand Tour. Kids helped clean and sort through two pounds of hard navy beans making sure we did not miss any pebbles or tiny dirt clumps that were trying to masquerade as beans. The beans soaked overnight in a kettle of cold water two days before the trip, then mother parboiled them an hour before they were baked. Shurley would eat beans only at the in-between stage, boiled but not baked and definitely not mushy because he only liked how they tasted if each bean rolled on the plate separately hard enough to not cling if they happened to bump.

Daddy got the car ready. Mother ironed clothes, did our hair and cooked. Crisp-coated fried chicken (wrapped in wax paper then into a brown paper bag), potato salad (chopped onions, green peppers, celery, hard-boiled-egg) and baked navy beans (sweet molasses, brown sugar plus a splash of Karo corn syrup), sometimes dropped biscuits which were my favorite but usually rolled biscuits that almost everyone else liked best. And ripe watermelon for dessert.

Just before bedtime Mother would straighten our hair, mine and Tish's, and she would straighten and marcel wave hers after all of us kids were in bed. Mother would lay out what we were going to wear for the trip and for play and for decent, three outfits for one day away. We went to bed early, willingly, because getting up in the dark for the trip was exciting, and my father usually had us on the road before dawn. I remember a car with a hand crank, Daddy would go to the front, kneel down on one knee, insert it at the center in an opening just above the bumper, grab the crank handle, twisting as he circled it down, round and briskly up with a strong pull; the engine sputtered unsure at least three times, while Mother's plea – be careful don't let it snap back, that thing could break your wrist – had us kids in the backseat to hold our breath.

Once we were on our way we'd fall asleep because it was still nighttime. We stopped along the way for a picnic and we always stopped at the same spring for crystal bright cold water. That was the beginning of our trip whether we were headed to Auburn or to my father's mother in Washington D.C.

Grandmother Diggs' house felt like country even though it was inside the small town of Auburn. It always seemed to me like a farmhouse from storybooks. Was it white? Did it have shutters? Or is that the way it felt at the end of the "long" 28-mile ride. It was smaller than our house, and it was closer to the street with a tiny front yard. In back a huge yard spread out at the bottom of the steep one-story slope Grandmother's house sat on. Her house had a wrap-around front side-porch big enough to hold all of the cousins when Aunt Belle and Uncle Lawrence with seven kids and all of us plus Uncle Al, Aunt Pauline, Kent, Don and Kathryn, who lived with Grandma, were there at the same time. That was a bunch of kids, 12-14, depending on who had been born or who already had died from Rheumatic Heart.

Grandma's house had kerosene lamps all of the time; at our house we just used kerosene lamps when our electricity had been shut off. Grandma's bathroom had a toilet that you reached way up high and pulled a chain to flush and the toilet was all that there was in the bathroom, no tub no sink; we washed up in a gray speckled enamel basin set on a wide shelf beside the bathroom door. When we stayed over a whole weekend, we took turns bathing in a round galvanized metal tub set up in the middle of the kitchen with all of the girl cousins sharing the first batch of heated water then all of the boys sharing the next. And Grandma posted someone at the closed kitchen door to protect privacy. My uncles and my father were the ones that had to fill the tub with steaming water; the brimming oval copper broiler, the cast-iron pots and kettles were too hot and heavy for the women to manage. As we took turns getting clean and playing pirate, new hot water was added, but we used what the first batch of children started out with until the bath was too scummed or chilled to expect the next cousins to get clean.

    We stepped out of the tub into a big cotton flannel double-thick sheet and shivered waiting for a grandmother rub-down. She wrapped us and rubbed us dry and warm.

    Three sets of cousins at Grandma's slept all over the house. Doubled and quadrupled up in the few beds. If you were still small and short you could arrange pillows and bedclothes on two straight wooden chairs pushed facing each other and spend the night in the best, best place of all. All the leftover children sprawled together on the dining room floor.

    The three Diggs girls had children, the only son, my Uncle Ed, had none. My Aunt Pauline had two sons and a daughter. My mother had two boys and two girls. And Aunt Belle, the youngest, had five daughters and two sons. My brothers, sister and I had a match in both sets of cousins. Richard and little Lawrence (Aunt Belle's sons), Kent and Don (Aunt Pauline's) were Shurley and Winthrop's ages. Aunt Pauline's Kathryn and Aunt Belle's Mary Elizabeth were my age. And Aunt Belle's Margaret Alice matched my sister Tish. By twos or pack we could be raucous. With three separate families together all us cousins got more freedom than in our own houses alone. The parents were under peer pressure, Let him go, Ritchie will look out for them, and besides it gave all the parents a break. Plus no matter how far (three blocks?) we wandered everybody in the neighborhood knew we were visiting Diggs kids, every adult would report and/or supervise us.

    There were times on a hot summer midday we played so hard that they put the whole bunch of us down for a nap, when those-children-been-just-run-ragged, and the adults needed some peace and quiet. These sessions started out mildly wild in choosing floor/bed arrangements, then melted into exhausted quiet reading whisper, and maybe even sleep. One afternoon I went downstairs ahead of the other kids, to sit at the kitchen table with Aunt Pauline, just watching blue jays and talking, happy I was the only one. She scraped two last scoops of the homemade peach ice cream into blue and white china saucers, one for me and one for her and whispered, If you hear Kent and Kathryn (her kids) come down, throw the dish out the window so they won't catch us eating it all up. I was licking the spoon slowly deliberate after each taste to make our secret snack last a long time. BLAM! some cousin's foot hit the top of the stairs and before Aunt Pauline could grab me if she had wanted to, my ice cream was sailing past the curtains, out the kitchen window, and into the deep valley backyard. One stunned second, and I knew I wasn't really supposed to, I folded into wailing sobs, inconsolable. And there stood Kathryn; she laughed and teased and leaned into her mother not even caring that the ice cream was gone.

I'd still hear how full Grandma's house was even in the dark after the final father's voice warned (again), you children settle down now or else: No ice cream; No picnic tomorrow; I'm coming in there! I MEAN IT. There was all that soft or noisy breathing, almost everyone had to roll, pull and tuck in their share of blanket, then one more whispered review. Or plan.

Once every year we visited our other grandmother in Washington, D.C., starting out in the middle of the night, too. But that grandmother's house felt mysterious, her city was out of my school books. There were no regular houses on Staple Street NE, there were two-story brick buildings. Grandmother Harris' downtown was The Smithsonian, Constitution Hall, Oh-oh, say can you see, by the dawnzerly light, and the White House!

I could not tumble out of the car and onto Grandmother's porch in Washington. I always had to wait for Daddy to choose the right door from a block-long line of all the same brick buildings, not houses, that all were exactly alike. Heavy gray stone cornices weighing down the front doors; a front stoop, steps to sit on but no porch (where would we play?), tiny squares of green grass and red geraniums jailed behind black shiny wrought-iron fence, each bar topped with a pointed wrought-iron crown, but not a fence for climbing because you would seriously wound, maybe impale yourself like King Arthur's knight or one of Robin Hood's men. A red brick building (house?) repeated as far as you could see on both sides of the street. Inside, Grandma Harris' house was dark and made me feel like touching the windowless walls to see if I could hear through my fingers. There was a whole family on the other side!

I don't know why we were allowed to refer to her as Aunt Tish not Grandma or Nana or "Two-Mamas." A grandmother whose name was Aunt Tish, down there where kids said things like youwall. Everyone, lots of relatives and even just friends, called her Aunt Tish. Her other son, Uncle Mordecai, we called Uncle Motor Car, at first because we thought we had it right and continued to sometimes say Uncle Motor Car because it had become a family story and everyone would laugh.

My grandmothers were both small, both soft-brown pretty, both widows (I had no grandfather), but they were not much alike. Rimless glasses pinched on her nose made my father's mother look like a school marm, not a grandmother. In her house people talked rather than laughing loud and telling afternoon stories that repeated with louder laughter into the night. And Uncle Mordecai, Daddy's brother, and Aunt Madeline had only one son, Oliver, who was Shurley's age, or older; he did not play and run like Syracuse and Auburn cousins did. In Washington I had to sleep in bed with Grandma (the one who did not let you even hold a hair comb in her kitchen let alone comb your hair there, a warning from mother before we even got to my father's mother's house). It was hard to fall asleep. I lay stiff working hard to not move close and touch, jounce the bed, disturb her rest. Grandmother Harris' good night sounded like a rules list, not that it was delivered scolding, just precise. You should have silk to wrap your hair at bedtime (I did); cotton or wool will break your hair off. Brush your teeth inside and out and use your toothbrush on your tongue (it's not a tongue-brush I would have muttered) at least four strokes at the very end. You should have slippers, Joan, to go to the bathroom. Or you can use the chamber pot. Did you put the lid on?

Down south we had to say: Yes ma'am, No ma'am, everyone did, even grownups, it was that part of the country's polite. Sometimes I'd forget, but Grandma's even-toned serious questions helped me remember where I was, most of the time.
      Yes what, Joan?
      Yes ma'm.

I wanted to be just like my big brother Shurley. I think it was because he would use big words as if we understood them. So we did. I see us sitting, not just us Harrises, but his friends his age too, sitting on the back porch listening to Shurley give lectures. They were lectures, but at the time it was just Shurley talking because that's what Shurley did. Sometimes with paper and pencil or chalk on the sidewalk to draw a graph, research percentages, or detail of a fly's eye the way it looked under a microscope. An exotic pagoda's tile roof. Or something he thought up to modify a model airplane kit he was working on. I was not allowed to touch the model airplanes, but I could watch if I did not talk or breathe hard enough to rustle the tissue paper that had to be delicately cut with razor blade and precisely laid on the fragile wood plane skeleton he'd shaped and assembled with airplane glue to fill the dovetailed balsa ribs of each model. All of his life he was inventing and teaching. Shurley's head would start bobbing and he'd say: centrifugal force, perpetual motion or suspended animation, and take off in animated explanation, carrying us along on his flight. I loved him so much.

Shurley built a car for the Soap Box Derby. It had to be according to official specifications. There was an official entry form filled and signed by him and by Daddy. And all of the work had to be done only by him. So it was. It took a long time, Shurley was intense as always, and as always nervously patient as he spelled out the process for me and all of the rest of the kids, his eager audience. The car was accepted, Bresee

Mother, baby Tish and Joan

Auto was sponsor and had a man drive Shurley and his car to Bellevue the day of the race. Mother took Tish and me to stand on the side of the hill and watch all of the fast kid-built cars wusshh past with barely time to identify who you knew. The loudspeaker boomed, Shurley Harris won his heat, and I was sure the announcement made him champion of the world. I started to run to the finish line to help them jump and yell, Mother balanced Tish on her hip, grabbed at my hand to hold me back to wait, to not interfere as he got ready for his next race. Winthrop was his pit crew, he did not need me there. I knew Shurley would win however many runs he had to, then I surely hoped Mother was going to let me race down to celebrate with the boys.

Three cars were there again, and down they all went, even faster than the first time. Wooooosshh to the finish. To race under the waving winning flag. And, Shurley's car was not first. That's not fair. What an unbelievable gyp this Soap Box Derby racing. I'd been ready for weeks to be in the coronation. I cried for myself, I cried for my brother, and I cried because I couldn't believe it. Now what will we do with the blue racer?

My mother used to say that Shurley was accident-prone. He did seem to have to have things bandaged more than the rest of us. Once he was steadying the board he was cutting to make his Soap Box car and he sawed off a big chunk of his knee. Once Shurley caught a second giant snapping turtle that he wanted to bring home to keep with the sluggish pet housed under our back porch, but the turtle caught hold of Shurley's finger instead of the stick (you always had to use as trick to make those big old turtles snap onto, then while their strong jaws were engaged you could pop them into the burlap sack you'd brought on the turtle hunt) and broke Shurley's finger, we think, because he could not bend it. Daddy carefully wrapped it with popsicle sticks as splint to hold it straight until it healed. And another time my brother came in holding his left arm funny, up against his chest, supported by his whole right hand spread out to cup the elbow. Shurley was in so much pain that he whispered. Mother sent him quick all by himself to the emergency room. Winthrop already had Rheumatic Heart and was on complete bed rest, there was no one else in our house or at the next-door neighbor's to stay with Win or go with Shurley. She wrapped his right hand and his left arm in place just the way he held them supported, whispered back to Shurley to tell him what to do; he walked away balancing his arm and hand wrapped close to his body. He was too big to sob; I thought that I was never going to see my brother Shurley again. Finally Mrs. Lynch came home and my mother got her to stay with Winthrop and me. Shurley came home with a real plaster-of-paris cast and a sling made of a large square of muslin that took specific folding instructions and proper safety pinning to support his arm and his cast until his broken arm healed.

  Shurley entered the derby three years in a row. Sometimes he won races and sometimes he didn't, but by that time he had a million ideas that were not on the page of required blueprint, and when the derby was over he'd spend another intense period breaking down and redesigning his car. After the derby it truly was Shurley's car. The year he built a sedan-like body that accommodated at least three or four kids he even put a roof on his car. Big kids folded themselves in half, and little kids begged for a ride pleeeeeease. And the low fast car went speeding down the hill, in the street, dangerously through the intersection at the bottom, whenever my mother and father were not at home.

Eventually some worried adult squealed on him, and Mother threatened that Shurley would have to take the car apart if they raced down our hill into traffic again.

So Shurley, Win and his friend Roy found a secluded enclosed place with hills and slopes that let them ride for miles with only one push. One great running shove at the top of the highest hill, just inside the tall wrought-iron gate, set them off on curved grade slopes that wound into and up gentler roads, twisted in through sharper grades so that the momentum allowed them to stay seated and concentrate on steering carefully, balancing their weight to not overturn through miles of shaded landscaped cemetery. I want to go, Ma-make-them-take-me-I'll-be-good. And she did. Because my presence could act as a brake on truly outrageous and reportable behavior? Because she was busy and did not need my help? I did not want to push my luck so I stood quiet and innocent close at Shurley's side following his every grumbling threat and instruction.

I-was-going-to-get-to-ride-down-real-hills-with-Roy-and-Shurley-and-Winthrop outside-of-the-neighborhood. Fast!

Woooophhh, it took my breath away. We whirled as fast as a real car, and there were not any windows. Hitting the bottom of a hill as my big brother held the steering wheel tight, turning into the right road for momentum to rush us up to the next crest. Woosh back rattling down. And up, and swirl back down again. Shurley drove or Roy, even Win, they took turns; I sat at the driver's back tucked between the big boys' knees in case we went so fast I could not hold on tight enough to stay seated. I tried not to scream but gleefully did, and my wails made the car lift from the ground and go much faster. Not Shurley, not Win, told me to stop it.

When I had had as much fun as I could stand I threw up all over everybody and everything, and we went home.

I did not get to go with the big boys any place again for a long long time. Me and my friends played in the backyard or on the front steps. The yard behind our house went straight back thirty feet, had a sudden small slope that dropped a couple of feet, then it leveled off as if nothing had happened and continued to a chain link fence. To begin real spring, after crocus had flowered and faded, six strong curved lilac bushes filled with color, hung blossoms across the fence that formed an arbor so thick, cozy and dark it was a playhouse. The smell of the flowers was in the air to mix with pretend fragrance of pretend tea and cakes.

Just after the lilacs and lilies of the valley bloomed, when school was out for vacation, the huckster's wagon would start to come by our house every week loaded with whatever was in season. The horse was not pretty, and I was sure he should not be. He had to pace slowly through the street, he did not belong in a race track stable. If he looked like Black Beauty or Man O' War he would be too fast to slow down and wait while my mother and the huckster bargained and talked of family. The huckster's horse had a heavy round rusted weight attached to his bridle with a rope long enough to anchor him in place, yet it let him sway his long nozzled head pulling grass and weeds from the tree lawn as he waited. Us little kids were allowed to sit lined up on the curb watching how his mouth worked as he slow nibbled. The huckster's horse stayed a long time. As soon as you heard, "Peaches Frrrresshcorn" the shopping crowd began to gather. At least one mother had said watch for the huckster today. We would stop playing and stop him. His wagon had a curved roof supported by four-by-fours at each corner with mesh onion bags, long strings of garlic and dried hot peppers, packs of garden seeds, nested pint and peck baskets hanging from them. The colors mixed and spilled from the roof down; he brought all of the vegetables and fruit that he grew himself, and then some. Mothers came out from up and down the block to surround his wagon, standing comfortably in the street two to three deep, leaning into the wagon from our driveway to prod and pick, poke and choose. Greeting, resting, making deals.

Mmm these are good, best I've tasted this summer I'll take four, how much are they? Got string beans today?

Where's Mrs. Hicks? Johnny's sick. Ohhhh I hadn't seen him. How much are these? my mother would bargain, I'll give you a quarter That's the last peck. Oh, go ahead, I'm on my way home now.

Sometimes, before he left, Mr. Sarafini would let someone feed his horse an apple. With my palm bent backwards, held high, and brave enough to not pull away from those huge soft nibbling lips.

Mother knew how to live easily on pennies, but some months were more uncertain than others. Sometimes several months in a row. Off and on we had to accept Soldiers and Sailors Relief food and sometimes (I am pretty sure) checks. This was welfare we got because Daddy served in World War I. He was wounded over in France. When I was little and worried after some terrible night fight, I used to think that his head wound explained why he drank. That is what made sense to me because liquor and beer never touched my mother's lips.

To get Relief we walked across town to a warehouse. With the proper card and papers checked off by the man, we'd wait until they loaded our share into Shurley's red cart. The food came in five-and ten-pound muslin sacks: flour, salt, corn meal, dark brown sugar, rice, elbow macaroni, and a brown cereal that was not finely ground and bleached like Cream of Wheat you could buy at the store, but that was okay because Nabisco's Cream of Wheat had this insulting picture of a darky in a white chef's hat grinning on the front of the box. The unbranded cereal was delicious hot with brown sugar mixed through and thick creamy evaporated milk poured over. I could even fix it for a snack in the middle of the day. We called it Tall, Dark and Handsome. I am not sure who made up that name, but all of us Diggs cousins called it that. The corn meal as hot cereal was called just plain mush, and corn meal as baked sweet bread was Johnny Cake. My mother made me an apron like hers, and I used a cookbook my friend Mrs. Stickney had given to me. The child on the cover could have been my age. The big red bow at the top of her blonde bob was tied exactly the same as my big red bow on my top braid, and the girl on the cover wore a white apron over her red dress as she concentrated on rolling the cookie dough flat. Each recipe was carefully worded and illustrated, so I only had to follow down the page step by step to make Johnny Cake from the yellow corn meal we got from the Soldiers and Sailors Relief. I used that book until the pages were tattered or glued together with splattered frosting and fudge.

When we made Johnny Cake I'd bake a portion in a toy pan to serve with what my grandmother called Cambric Tea, hot water, milk, a rounded spoonful of sugar, and no tea. It looked like the real tea with milk that my Canadian-born grandma always drank only from thin porcelain cups. Grandmother declared that the cup's thinness made the tea taste the only way that tea should taste. To sip tea from anything else made the sipper a bit of a ruffian.

Used books, used clothes, used furniture sustained us. Use it up, wear it out, make it do or do without. That is how most people lived, back then. All of our clothes were made, remade, passed down, or bought at the rummage shop. My mother could go into the most disorganized dark shop, look at the tallest messy pile on the biggest table, reach in and pull out an imported Harris Tweed coat in perfect size and condition. My mother and Aunt Belle loved Saturday. Every single Saturday morning Isaba/evelyn got to run away from home to laugh and play together at The Rum.

Rum was our word for all rummage shopping, shops, church sales, flea markets, tag sales and what-not. It is still the family name for secondhand stores and shopping. The Rum. Isaba/evelyn would go by bus to do the Salvation Army store or their favorite Rum, Miss Stickney's Shop. When they walked into either shop, they were greeted, welcomed as family. Miss Stickney would often pull some hidden item from below the counter. Something special that she had set aside with Mrs. Harris or Mrs. Williams in mind. She knew all of our sizes and Mother's taste almost as well as Mother did. Mother had a keen sense of style that she had developed some place within her own working-class classy family, then cultivated it by paying attention to the fashion magazines that she found and brought home from the Rum, along with all of the clothes that we wore and most of the household and knickknack stuff that we had. When Mother took us walking through Addis or Flah's or Milgrim's, those were the clothes that made me feel at home. Rich velvet textures, coarse woven monochromatic tweed, hand-(not machine turned) crocheted laces. I owned the Melton wool navy blue coat, with half-belt and small velvet collar that the Addis child mannequin showed. Mother bought the matching coat and hat with rolled ties, at two different Rums, months apart. Just looking, my mother nodded, window-shopping at Flah's. She had taste and an incredible knack for making us look moneyed.

Whenever Mother and Aunt Belle were at The Rum on Saturdays, we were supposed to stay in the house, complete our weekly chores and not fight. Usually we did not fight, and we stayed indoors. We almost always sort of tore the house apart. We needed forbidden material for the adventures we made up. Everything we invented seemed to require furniture up-ended and living-room sofa cushions propped for barricades or walls. And we had to have blankets and comforter dragged down from everyone's bedroom (including Mother and Daddy's) to make roofs and doorways for dark caves or secret hideouts. We played furiously, with one eye on the clock, then frantically started our jobs twenty minutes before we figured Mother would get home.

We listened to the radio program Nila Mack's Let's Pretend, dramatized classic fairy tales, while Mother was away. I sat face close to the radio, and shoulder touching close to

Shurley and Winthrop. They were bigger brave boys and the loud terrible voice of Bluebeard was authentic. It did not matter that I knew she'd eventually live happily ever after, when Bluebeard's low evil words warned: Don't unlock that door while I am away! I was sure that something brutal could happen to me and to his silly new wife.

    Going to The Rum continues a passion for my sister Letitia and me, in Syracuse, or my daughter Letitia and me, in Atlanta, every time I go to see them. It's an Isaba/evelyn tradition even though they are named for my father's side of the family. Rums don't have the dank smell they did when I was small. When I was small there were mountains of clothes jumbled high on tables broad enough for Ping Pong. If Mother and Aunt Belle took us with them we played pretend games under the tables, or read books that we chose from the book section in the back of the room. Except for having to appear to have a sleeve and arm measured we did not pay attention to the stuff until we were back home squealing and claiming dibs on certain items from each week's loot. Mother could look at a dress and redesign it in her mind while I twisted and preened. Oh, look, this could be...? And what if or maybe...? My mother could add a hand smocked or fagotted yolk, change gussets and puffed sleeves, tuck and hem. In the transformed accordian-pleated sheer white organdy dress (from The Rum) I was Shirley Temple, all of America's darling. Dimples and all.

    The Shirley-Temple-curls were put in

with hot curling irons. Back then people washed up every morning but took baths only once a week. The long slow Saturday bath had time for scrubbing and even time to turn onto my stomach to courageously swim the rough English Channel just like Florence Chadwick, then step boldly out (to wipe up the puddled bathroom floor). I had to hurry downstairs because my hair needed to be combed out while it was still damp, or it would dry impossibly knotted, snagging it from its roots. Mother settled on the painted bright yellow wooden chair. I went and got the oak foot-stool to sit nestled between my mother's knees, a towel draped across my shoulders and an open jar of hair grease held high with my right hand as she combed my hair into fourteen small square sections. Dabbing each section dry with a towel, massaging Dixie Peach with Bergamot into my scalp, she combed through my kinked hair, twisted tight one finished square and moved on to the next knotty uncombed place. I would scrunch up my shoulders, wince at the snarls, pull away in pain causing more pain, because I had snatched against her strong sure hands, and against her patience. Sit still. Don't twist your head. And will you please keep the grease where I can reach it.

When every section was combed smooth, towel-dried, oiled, Mother put two straightening combs on the gas jet and a large, folded, heavy white linen napkin on the ledge of the white enamel stove. We waited until the combs were hot just right. She would rub the back edge of the comb between the pad-folded cloth. Move the comb close to her nose and lips to sense how much heat there was. Strike it one more time on the napkin, then pull it down through one layer, of one section of my hair. But if a few strands of hair are still damp, Sizzle-spit! Water pops on to my scalp, scares me and I jump straight against the hot steel comb. Sometimes, I'd get a really deep burn and have a burn's scab on the tip of my ear that I would lie to white folks about until it was completely healed.

Sometimes, my mother and I sat silent in the rhythm of the comb. Sometimes she would softly croon: Listen to the lambs. Listen to the lambs, All-a-cryin' or some other Saturday-night-kitchen lullaby. Or, maybe I would have a convoluted tale of school to tell, that kept my head bobbing with the adventure. Joan. Please! Hold your head up.

When I was a little kid, I wanted long hair. It did not have to be soft or curly. I liked black hair best and kinky was good as long as God would grant my prayer for long hair, hair that would please-please hang down to my waist. All right, not all the way to my waist, just touching my shoulders would be grand. Kinky and thick enough for the weight of it to give motion as I tossed my head or when I ran Red Rover in the school playground. I wanted long hair and had only enough to fold into very short braids. (What I secretly coveted was Dee Dee Jeffries' hair.) Dee Dee had black kinky hair, with each braid (of three!) as thick as my wrist, and heavy so it hung swaying to the middle of her back.

All of my cousins could go grow long hair.

Aunt Belle's and Aunt Pauline's kids. At church if I sat behind my cousin Mary Elizabeth I would dream entranced by her straightened hair touching so lightly on her back that she probably didn't feel it or think about it all during the whole hour of Sunday School. Probably it did not make a bit of difference to her that part of her hair separated and fell in front of her shoulder, and part of it rested in back as she moved her head forward to study the Bible card picture of Jesus with a circle of blond babies at his bare feet. My hair, even straightened, did not reach the top of my neck and was definitely not tossable. My mother's hair was way longer than mine, and worn in marcel waves. Plus, the other thing, I was the only one in the whole family with a short common name: Falstaff Lionel Harris, Evelyn Claracy Diggs Harris, Shurley Holton Harris, Winthrop Sterling Harris. (It did not make up for anything that my mother gave me her first name as my second. No one ever cared about middle names. Except, maybe, Franklin Delano Roosevelt. Mary McLeod Bethune.) And they even waited until after me to name my baby sister Letitia Elaine, absolute proof that I was left on the Harris doorstep with a note pinned to my bunting giving my plain first name but not warning them that my hair would always (all ways) be short!

When I was a little kid I secretly longed, prayed for, three kinky hanging braids. I needed long hair for when I recited pages-long The Creation by James Weldon Johnson for an AME Zion Sunday School skit. Still, my mother looked patiently straight at me to listen, again and again and again to each sentence, each verse, each word as I memorized and rehearsed. In the kitchen, in the living room, or beside my bed in the night.

I wanted long hair when I was a little girl. What I had was: a warm kitchen, an oak footstool, and my mother singing down over me as she croquignoled hot tiny Shirley-Temple-curls into my short straightened hair that we would wrap in a silk scarf. To hold for Sunday morning.

When I was grown with young children of my own I started wearing my hair cut short. On purpose. My natural did not rival the full-blown raging crowns of young people, but it felt as beautiful and important. In the beginning I didn't know that one of my best reasons for having my hair very short and very kinky was going to be barbershops. God, black barbershops are wonderful. They are great because: this is one place that is ours; not much money is involved; grown men are not only allowed to play here, they are expected to; and there is even hope.

Barbershops are supposed to be exclusively male, but nowadays, mothers as well as fathers are allowed to escort young sons. And, although many black men are not happy about black women cutting off whatever length of hair they are able to grow, women like me, who choose to wear our hair short and nappy, come into the barbershop to get it shaped.

The truly recalcitrant doubter is impressed by a professional cut, and most are ready to admit that when it is done well, It is smart! I love the rumbling of men who are black. Their language, their voice, the pitch of their laughter. In the barbershop black men are who they are. Wise, funny, compassionate, outrageous, silly, pedantic, rich, misinformed, brilliant, creative and at ease. They are so beautiful. If you are a kid or a woman and you sit very still in the barbershop, the men will let you listen. They will continue to carry on as if you are not even there. So, on any given day, at the barbershop, I feel privileged. There are so many stories that get told.

VII

On most Sunday nights we all listened to the radio: Jack Benny, Eddie (Rochester) Anderson, Mrs. Nussbaum; Fred Allen, Allen's Alley; Charlie McCarthy and Mortimer Snerd (listening to the radio you didn't notice Edgar Bergen's lips move as much as when he was on the movie screen; the radio is what made him a famous ventriloquist).

Inner Sanctum was a scary radio program that Winthrop and I were not usually allowed to stay up and listen to. But once in awhile if the whole family snuggled around the radio and the narrator had already leered: Welcome to the Inner Sanctum, I might be squeezed into the corner of Mother's overstuffed chair, and perhaps Winthrop was too small to be noticed cross-legged beside Shurley on the floor, so sometimes we were not dismissed to bath and bed. Which felt great while I was safe in the chair with my mother, but after the program we left the living room and there was Shurley nipping at my heels with maniacal laughter as I raced step by step up the stairs to stay out of his scary transformed big brother threat. Whatever demon was the Inner Sanctum protagonist turned a thousand times worse imitated to perfection by Shurley. He could recreate everything. The slow chilling creak in the front door hinge of the mansion. The innocent tenor of the stupidly trusting visitors, the engaging sneak as the villain first tricked them. The cackle of triumph. Then silence. From the dark, my head buried beneath blankets, I did not know if he had left or was just standing there waiting.

    I suppose that if I had not mixed giggles into my terror trying to grab the bedroom light chain, perhaps my parents would have taken me seriously and come upstairs to save me. They would only mildly scold, muffled from way down in the kitchen. My mother and father did not dash up the steps to rescue.

    Did Lights Out, the horror tales radio program, come on on Sunday evening? Its ominous organ theme song sent Winthrop, Tish and me scattering before the creepy guttural announcer began the evening's tale. Shurley was allowed to stay up and listen to the ghost stories all by himself. He was the only one in the living room late on that night, I could not really hear the radio, but we all knew how true the stories were, imagination filled the picture in my mind. I was upstairs in my bed completely under the covers, just waiting, just waiting to hear Shurley's footsteps end the weekly grim tale. He listened huddled in the radio's story until the last commercial sign off and theme. Then, he had to click the radio dial, turn off the table lamp and hit the bottom stair and the hall switch all within one safe second. My big brother Shurley was fast. He could take the stairs three at a time! My job was to hide in my bed holding my breath from the moment I heard him jump on that first step until he dove from his doorway to his own blankets. When I heard his bedspring creak, then could hear my brothers' voices begin to mumble soft and we were safe.

Safe, until Shurley (sometimes with his cohort, our cousin Little Lawrencey) was in charge of all the cousins on a Saturday while Aunt Belle and Mother went to the Rum. They would terrorize us with their own invention based on Lights Out, Inner Sanctum or Nila Mack's Saturday Morning Fairy Tale villains. Shurley and Lawrencey painstakingly developed strange cackling voices and designed dark costumes, some with built-in hunchback, from the junk trunk in the attic. Then they memorized or improvised on dialogue from any of the stories. Shrouded within a full-length dark hooded cape, Shurley would attack, holding a flashlight just below his chin to cast transmuting shadow up onto the face of Werewolf-Jeckle/ Hyde-Frankenstein monster, loping after us in stumbling menace. Each and every Saturday we would die a hundred deaths when we were discovered hidden in the corner of the coal bin, scooched against the wall under the bed or balanced-tucked behind hats, bags and blankets on the top of the bedroom closet's high wooden shelf. For these dastardly deeds, Shurley had a soul mate in Little Lawrence and they would retire to the boys' bedroom to plot horrible wickedness. Lawrencey was actually closer to Winthrop in age, but Winthrop didn't have a stomach for mental torture even before he got sick. All of us girl cousins would use the time that Shurley and Lawrencey were behind closed doors getting ready, to try to plan routes of escape, mild counterattack and safe hideaways. We shrieked and raced and giggled. The boys always won.

When I was seven years old I started sleepwalking every once in a while. What were you doing down there, Joan?, and I am at the top of the stairs in the hall outside my bedroom wearing pajamas. I don't know. Mother? It is dark and the house is still. Everyone is asleep? She turns on the light. I wake up a little more and can see my father through the open bedroom door. Raised on an elbow, from his side of their bed he wonders the same question, Joan, what were you doing down there? More awake. I go in the bathroom to pee. Then come out. To listen. Half asleep. My mother describes hearing me descend the stairs, move into the living room, through the kitchen and dining room. Softly pushing things around. I don't know. (I had been sound asleep and not even dreaming. I don't dream.) Mother puts me back to bed. I snuggle in not awake enough to even wonder or worry about what they said has just happened.

>I still never dream.
>(Almost never.)
>It is all the same,
>that emptiness within sleepwalking,
>amnesia and
>dreamless sleep.

No matter.
I am inside a Steady White Noise Completely. It fills my nostrils, my ears (no real sound), all my skin pores. With eyes closed (no images) it rests against the eyelids; if they opened it would suction onto my moist eyeballs

Slightly balloons my vagina to the cervix with no pressure
If I open my mouth, it would pour in there gently puff my lips away from my teeth, flow down my throat to my larynx, but not gag me.
No urgency.
Just space
White Noise is under the soles of my feet.

And Now
And now today
and now This Night
Wide Awake. Not a dream And now.
No matter how desperately I twist and scrunch to fasten my shoulder to my ear, I can not get away from the woosh and air of my father's
Come on come on

I use both hands to push him off.
No.
No. Now I know.
Breathe, breathe. Stop screaming.
I can't breathe or run or turn on the lights
    I can't stop it
        Stop it!
           Turn on the lights try to turn on the lights and breathe. Just breathe. Don't run. Don't scream
      again
I scream
I can hear it turn on,
the lights don't run
Get out of bedhurrybreathe

> Get out of the bedroom
> it is (BREATHE) not happening now
> turn on the light
> TURN ON THE LIGHT

I am out in the hall. I can't get the light on my body remembers, so I throw up to stifle a scream. He is dead! He has been dead! You are an old woman!

he is dead he has been dead you are an old woman

he is dead he has been [breathe it] dead you are
      an old woman he is dead I am
        I am an old woman
          and he is dead.

Around 4 a.m. I can dial a phone. 3913912.

With my lights still not on, Rape Crisis Hotline allows me to breathe deep sobs breathe long .... silences until I cry out of the eye of the flashback and she knows. I don't tell her about his orgasm but I tell her I am alone.

After the phone I can do something about the smell. I wipe up the pool of thick off-color vomit, tie the soiled washcloth and dirty rags tightly in a black plastic bag that I carry into the middle of the night backyard.

Once I know, each flashback stays constant for weeks, just above and behind my ear. His voice Come on come on come on hot and deep but I cannot get way because he is stronger. His Sound his Air, not mine.

Even now, years past the orgasm flashback, when I write it or when I tell it now as memory (and under my control) my body removes in quieted terror a little nausea is held high in my throat but, first, the burning ear and the muscles of my left shoulder strain up.

I lose time.

Whole blocks of time, while I am still here. I know it only after the fact, after I slowly return. There is a thought: Oh. I am coming back now. I look up. Here I am. I have been away. I am never sure of how long. I sometimes note how long it seems. A few days, a month, a moment. That was possible to conceive, but to consider 52 years was agony. My amnesia described such profound loss. I could not bear it. I did not want it. There was nowhere to place it and feel any way except insane. How Could I Not Know? For months I deliberately hid the amnesia as zealously as it had hidden the incest. There was more shame in being dumb.

Falstaff Harris, Artist, Is Dead

Falstaff Harris of 1053 E. Fayette St., operator of the Falstaff Harris art studio at that address, died yesterday in the V.A. hospital.

Born Oct. 25, 1894, in Washington, D. C., Mr. Harris was graduated from Armstrong Technical High School in that city in 1913.

He attended Pratt Institute of Art in New York City and the Syracuse University College of Fine Arts. He was awarded the Leavenworth prize in art at S. U.

During World War I Mr. Harris was chief draftsman with the AEF. He was employed as artist for Keith's Theater from 1923 to 1930.

In the second World War Mr. Harris was a draftsman and tool designer in defense plants.

He painted murals in numerous local homes and night clubs and also in the children's ward of Onondaga Sanatorium. Mr. Harris was former president of the Dunbar Association.

Surviving are his widow, Mrs. Evelyn Diggs Harris; two sons, Shurley Holton Harris of Mattydale and Falstaff Harris Jr.; two daughters, Mrs. Robert Southgate of Cleveland, Ohio, and Miss Letitia E. Harris of Florence, Italy; a brother, Mordecai U. Harris of Washington, D. C., and four grandchildren.

Services will be conducted at the Garland Bros. Funeral Home at 1 p.m. Thursday, the Rev. Emery Proctor officiating. Burial will be in Oakwood Cemetery.

Friends may call from 2 to 4 and 7 to 9 p.m. tomorrow.

FALSTAFF HARRIS

Tish would say Joan-you-don't-remember-anything whenever she told a great story. Joan-you-don't-remember-anything is the chorus at every loud, laughing family gathering. Remembering never mattered, I would gleefully accept the long-ago details of my clever or cute or stupid. I didn't remember the details, but it felt as good as being there, I might actually recall a fragment, a sound, an autumn color. We giggled, hooted and laughed all of us together. I wasn't the one telling the story, but that was just the way I was. I was always sort of shy, and I was forgetful, that is who I am. Neither aspect tragic nor outstanding in the way I brightly acted them out. A good listener, a fantastic audience. I am loud-laughing, raised-eyebrows ready for any great punchline you belt out into mixed company. I get it I get it. In fact I often got it during anticipation and build-up line. I was always included and delighted by everything my bright baby sister said. One evening when we three old women (our friend Marilyn, me, and Tish) danced in memories' foibles so loud and happy that our stomachs hurt, Tish announced, Joan, the reason you don't drink is cause you don't have to, any witness would think all three of us had had wine. Which set us sailing to higher gales of laughing and choking and having such great fun, remembering.

Remembering early summer. Night time, Aunt Belle's house on Washington Street. My mother, father, Aaron and Margie Bagby, Aunt Belle and Uncle Lawrence are inside the house playing Mah Jong. We are outside playing hard.

Fast. Running. Shrieking. Laughing falling down.

It was Hide and Seek after dark with wonderful undiscoverable places to tuck into. I know that I am playing. I know that I am panting because it is scary and soooooo much fun. And you have to be quiet and still and not let It find you. Don't giggle. Don't breathe. Hide! I am running far, fast as the wind, to a genius-secret-dark-dark-no-one-has ever-thought-of-this-before hiding place. Little Lawrencey, Mary Elizabeth, Claire, Shurley, Winthrop, Rosalyn Bagby Olley Olley Octen Free Olley Olley Octen Free come on, Joan. That meant that I had won! I held my breath quietest I found the darkest dark place I hid Best.

No matter as fast as I ran, as hard as I breathed (or held my breath). Laughed and yelled, squeeeeeeeealed. There was also floating slow action. Dull film scrimmed my eyes. Hollow echo filled my ears and I wanted to come full stop and ask immediately Hey, what is this? But we were all ear-shattering gleeful hot fun and I was afraid to be the only one

This floating happened more than once. Sometimes, when it was quiet, at night, on the front porch steps, I tried to ask Winthrop or Shurley if they ever felt like that, but their long drawn-out naaaah told me to stop asking

I must be the only one. Forget it, forget I stopped asking but I always knew, always remembered, the floating above non-frightening time.

VIII

My mother would call out after me when I was 5, 6, 9 years old, Joan? Walk. I said walk! Stop running can't you ever walk? And I couldn't. I had to run, because it felt right. All the time. Everywhere. The running took my breath away and replaced it with air whisking across my eyelashes, past my ears with the sound of a soft wishhhhhhhhhhhhh.

The oldest tree on Renwick was right at our back-door steps. The cigar tree was also the only one that flowered, curious-shaped white blossoms with carefully painted purplish brown lines and a dot of bright yellow that bled through the bent mouth of each small curled flower. The cigar tree did not grow straight up and tall, it was tall in spite of the fact that it leaned at a sixty five degree angle. Which meant it was pitched to climb. Then I would relax, hiding quietly above the unsuspecting.

Our slanted-trunk tree had broad plain pale green leaves all summer; in the autumn they turned not very interesting yellow-brown to die. It was the maple tree in front of my house and the maple trees in the Old Lot, all the maples scattered through our neighborhood, that burst into fall treasures to collect, sort and press for mounting as children's decoration.

By winter The Old Lot was entrance to a home-made toboggan run that Junior Livingston's father used to create as soon as temperature stayed below freezing. That hill was higher than a house was tall, it sloped from Renwick Avenue level down to the backyard edge of Castle Street's bottom end and Mr. Livingston would flood the freezing path as wide as two and a half driveways. Room enough to not even have to wait to take turns. Broad-top-gatewayed for takeoff at will on corrugated cardboard scrounged from Mr. Johnson's grocery store or boxes purposefully hoarded in your own basement or attic. We would rush everyday after school.

Flopped belly, slipped bottom. Or leaning back, long line together 8, 12, 16 legs grabbed in a train. Why didn't we freeze caught wet snowsuit stiff mid-motion? Because we zoomed downhill faster than wind laughing loud and the run back up raised our body temperature one-million-twenty-two degrees.

On school days you could take only one quick slide at lunchtime. Except, one day Tish and I forgot it was noon and we raced up and down and up and down and up and down and up and, we were both officially tardy back to school. Being late, like being absent, required a note from your mother. We were so late it was shameful (could it have been an hour? I have no idea) but Mrs. Amdursky made me go home to get the note right then and there. While I sniffle-bawled the terrible truth that it wasn't my fault, because Tish said we had plenty of time. I wanted to leave and...but Tish said, that's only the first bell...and we ran all the way! but Ma, I didn't even hear no bell at all. My mother scowled appalled and scolding, Joan, you are the oldest and you knew full well what time it was when you left home. She rubbed her palm across my wet face and handed me clean clothes; long-leg underwear tucked in lisle stockings and my dry play clothes snowsuit. Mother let me lean against her body as I sobbed repentant. And sent me back to school with a note of apology and promise.

Day after day. After school and after Saturday chores, The Old Lot was teeming with screaming and lots of loose falling-down bodies. Kids from every block in the neighborhood came to slide into the night. Until mothers began calling our full Christian names and threatened that they, the mothers, would follow their voices out into the dark. To the top of the hill.

And get us.

In winter, the electric bills were often a problem. Mother knew that it was more a question of saving enough rather than making enough, especially during the Depression. So besides The Rum, she had to figure out many ways to get by.

We used our emergency kerosene lamps with trimmed wick and polished glass chimney in case of a shut-off. Or sometimes we hid so the light man couldn't get in to throw the switch. Daddy was at work and not a part of it. Mother would warn that this would be the day the Illuminating

Company man came, and the company truck was easily identified. On that day we did not go into the yard to play. When he knocked on the door the scurry had to be completely muffled. For added intrigue my brothers and I would scuffle across the room to press our backs to the wall beneath the picture window in case the serviceman was eager or clever enough to peer through suspicious silence. Without a sound we enacted G Men, Nancy Drew or our own secret society, grinning broadly, smothering laughter to tears. It was a game and when we won, I felt heroic. It got tense when they would come in two's and cover the back and front doors and check the basement windows. The successful delay was no more than a few days, but sometimes that was all that my mother and father needed to scrape together the small amount of the bill. If the service men came back and caught us off-guard everyone was shamed, even the workmen. In the Great Depression they were forced to cut off too many families a lot like their own.

If the gas was about to be shut off the routine was the same, though success was not critical. We could live a long time without gas. In the kitchen, catty-corner from the wooden ice box, was a small square black four-lid wood stove that we used for extra heat in the winter. When the gas was cut off we used it for everything no matter the season. Our oval copper boiler fit over two lid openings and with the four-quart aluminum tea kettle plus a black encrusted iron pot we heated enough water for laundry or for a skimpy warm bath. The oven baked biscuits, warmed leftover catsup-sweetened beans, and dried puddle-soaked shoes that I never remembered until everyone screamed: Burning Rubber!

If we were without gas in the summer and had to burn wood for cooking, a million times a day, mother pleaded, Close the dining room door! as she tried to keep the heat confined. In the winter the little stove was fine supplement to the furnace. Coal bought by the ton, was delivered swift through a chute into the coalbin, a dark walled corner of the basement with one small window that the Huber Coal man would prop up to open its hinged wood frame. He stood on top of the truck-load with a shovel sending one ton of rock-size black coal clattering down the steel chute he attached to the rear of his truck like a funnel. His truck bed tilted at a 45-degree angle, for the coal to glide in. The pile was enormous, higher than I was tall; the unloading took a long time. I never understood how we could ever run out before spring. The times that we did and we had also run out of money, the small kitchen stove was the heat that we had for the whole house. We lived tucked in one room sometimes for weeks. Mother use rolled up newspaper or folded rags to chink the drafty windows, brought rag rugs in for the linoleum kitchen floor. And kept towels or wool fabric pushed up against the inside and outside kitchen doors. We slept in double socks and hooded jackets with lots of coats piled on top when we'd used all the blankets. During the night if I needed to use the bathroom, I'd stay put, fall back to sleep and wet the bed, too snug to leave until forced into morning. I dreaded the frozen space between my warmed bed upstairs and our black kitchen stove. I had to swirl the blanket quickly around, across my shoulders, over my head and down to my toes and hold it high enough to not trip. Dash through the hall down the steps, to stand close at the side of the hot stove that Daddy had stoked twenty minutes before we were called to get ready for school. The kitchen warmed the day's start. My chilled fingers fumbled all the tiny underwear buttons into their small buttonholes, pressed my brown lisle stockings into garter clasp. I finished dressing, completely inside a warm blanket tent.

Fuel to heat the stove we gleaned from Huber Coal Company's yard and Wilson Lumber Company when we could not buy it. Both were only a few blocks away. The coal yard was open and anyone who needed to could pick up or shovel the spill anytime as long as they did not get in the way of the rumbling coal delivery trucks that pulled in and out filled high to almost spilling. Shurley pulled me to Huber's on our Radio Flyer sled then he let me help fill the bushel basket with coal to the top. Maybe I'd help push the sled back home, most of the time he would pull me and the coal. For kindling without money, Mother would send us to the lumberyard that was farther away, and Shurley invented a way to carry more wood than we could have gotten in a basket on a sled. It took longer and sometimes other kids joined us. Glenn and Roy, maybe my cousin Mary Elizabeth. After searching out just the right length (about 4 to 6 feet long) 2 x 4's, we would break wooden laths into short pieces and begin piling them neatly balanced across the long 2 x 4's. Checking to test weight and placement as the load grew. The trick was to break and add more laths until two of us could lift them like a stretcher. Then we formed a parading caravan swaying and teetering down the street in the road, close to the curb so we would not have to shift and adjust at each intersection. Of course there were spills. Especially if we decided to race! Are all the stacks equal? Line up. Wait! No cheating, if a car comes everybody stop. No starting again until I say so. Ready. Set. Go!

The sound of crunched new-fallen snow and brittle footsteps. Especially days we had taken so long at Wilson's that the sky was darkening. Not quite night, not scary dark, I could still see our smoke breath rise up in quick puffs, because of how fast we were trotting with the weight of our wooden litter.

Upstate New York had snow that lasted on the ground from November to March, maybe April. Temperatures could drop below freezing and stay there for days without our noticing it much. Once it got cold the combination of snow piling and packing was usual. As winter moved into January there would be enough freezing, then slight warm up then freezing, for the top layer of ten or twelve inches to form a solid crust two inches hard. I was light enough to walk on top without sinking. When the winds were high the air filled with cutting snow blowing almost parallel to the ground I would have to twist and adjust direction leaning forward or backing into sharp howl: I struggled bravely into bitter wind across my Alaska tundra with pretend goggles to prevent snow blind and only one broken invisible snow shoe. Alone. Under darkened sky. Sometimes my high rubber boot would break through the ice surface trapping my leg hip deep and dangerously twisted, Come on boy, come on Wolf. Mush. Get me out of here. Mush. Come on boy you can do it, ya gotta help me. If I don't get free I'm a goner. Puullllll. I was in a desperate journey to reach the 616 Renwick Avenue Outpost. There wasn't much time: to have lunch, pick up Joan Crawford and Dolores and get back to school before the bell rang. Together we would plot and plan, running all the way back to school. After school we could change out of school clothes to meet in my back yard where Shurley'd been helping build an igloo. Daylight was short, there was never enough time, Joan had to go back home as soon as the street light came on but our mothers usually gave Dolores and me permission stay out in the dark a little longer. Our mothers considered the adjoining backyards as one yard, we were all playing together.

Every child had school clothes and play clothes. It was important not to use one set for the other. When we were in the midst of some long play project I did not have to have mother remind me, Change your clothes, Joan. On those days I knew exactly where I had stuffed everything I wore for after school. My old snowsuit was hanging to dry from last night, out in the back hall. And I hoped my old shoes were near the stove. I rushed to get all ready to be first outside. It was too quiet, and the time dragged, did they get in trouble? Will their mother let them come? It was cold, with no one else outside. My big brother showed up later after he had finished with his own friends. Me and Dolores and Joan needed him. We had made a six foot circle of chipped square huge snowballs and stacked them three blocks high already. That took two days! We even had to cart bushel baskets of snow all the way from Dolores' yard and from the Old Lot. We took turns being the Huskies, harnessed carefully taut within the sled's pull rope. We tried everything to form our igloo roof. We cut with the edge of Daddy's snow shovel and the edge of a spade, I even snuck in the house and got the serrated bread knife. No matter how we sculpted the snow blocks they would not hold and curve into a round roof top. Nothing worked.

We made millions of successful snow forts. Sometimes, two forts facing each other started with winter's first soft wet snow of any depth. The straight fort walls built tall enough for ambush, adequate for ducking out of the way of an attack, took almost every child in the neighborhood to be builders. And opposing armies. We would take afternoon into evening with a truce declared so we could build up our ammunition supply. Hours of making snowballs, yelling from within walled fortress, giggling exaggerated numbers to the enemies' side. We would stop to count each snowball over and over a hundred times, to keep track, and to take a break from molding and patting wet snow dumps. We would play until our mittens were soaked and freezing, go inside and exchange that pair for dry. If a raging battle obtained we would run out of mittens and pull two pair of socks on our hands for thumbless mittens.

Chilled to the bone from the outdoors' air. So hurt and cold I'd start crying, I would not be able to take my boots off all by myself. The third finger on my right hand would have turned white and numb. You should have known better, Joan. My mother's stern admonition. Don't tell me you didn't realize you were this wet! Are you trying to catch pneumonia? Give me that shoe. She jerked it off impatiently and arranged my dead wet clothing across the warm furnace register. I just stood. Sobbed. Moaned and sniffled. In too much pain to recall just minutes ago I'd been happily yelling at the top of my lungs. By the time we'd huddled by the kitchen stove and Mother had finished sucking her teeth at our foolishness, we were okay. Except for chilblains and I don't even hear that word anymore. Was it frostbite? We only called them chilblains. The treatment felt terrible but somehow proper in the same way that painting burning iodine on a cut made you brave. Mother approached chilblains with serious caution. Anyone of us kids without the painful aching was instructed to gather a brimming full basin of snow and bring it into the warm kitchen.

I'd been having fun and the next thing I knew, stars are out. And here I am headed in the house bent and limping. How could my whole foot be stiffened numb and shrieking pain all at the same time? No way could I take off my wet shoe, ever. Each one of us had chilblains sometime during each winter, sometimes more than once. Out of our experience came empathy that turned each and every one of us into a willing assistant caretaker.

Go fill the basin with snow, hurry.

One of us was out the door quickly, then back standing at sympathetic attention. Hunched on the kitchen chair wrapped in a big old wool blanket warmed and dried beside the stove, I cry louder for more attention, pleased that my biggest brother has stooped to play nurse for me, without calling me big baby or grumbling that I was spoiled. Once when he had chilblains, Shurley let me ease his big sopping shoes and galoshes off. I kept my eyes lowered afraid he would be embarrassed when he realized he'd said yes I could, he was like Gary Cooper biting a bullet. Mother coaxed-forced you to lower your poor foot into the icy mound of melting snow in the enamel basin. It didn't help. It hurt! But was the only safe sure cure to save your toes and to eventually ease the throbbing of chilblains. No matter which one of us it was we filled the kitchen air with broken sobbing. No matter which one of us it was, when our feet were better we never remembered to come in from a snow fight/play before we were soaked again and frozen.

In the evening Mother would build up the wood fire for cooking and for warmth. After play, before homework we would thaw out huddling close to that stove.

We hear his key fumbling to open the front door. Shhhh, Daddy's here. All us kids crowd up the stairs. Fast! Dragging our clothes and towels, at the top Winthrop and me stop. Listen very quietly. Pressed forward we strain to hear a reason he's come home so late?

Evelyn! My father is shouting, she's right in the next room. His footsteps move toward the kitchen. No noise. Mother is trying not to answer him. He's deciding how to try to act, fish t'night? Something about fish? It is not even Friday? Is that what he said?

It is quiet upstairs and downstairs. Maybe we will quietly get through the night. I cannot hear anything. Now, I can smell fish frying and try to remember if there is a different smell to mackerel and pike. Listen. I am pretty sure he has been drinking. If he wasn't I would go down to help scrape off the last scales of the fish. I used to be scared to touch slimy fish skin, now I help scale them before Mother rolls them in cornmeal for frying. There is a special knife and a tricky grip to hold the fish tail tight, always scraping against the grain.

None of us would go down until we were called to set the table. When my father came drunk, the smell of liquor changed the air. Meals were dangerous. It was best to not talk, just eat, be quiet. That did not always work. Just because he had been drinking the same, did not mean that he was going to be the same drunk person each time he walked through the door. At times it was clear that he wanted you to tell him about play or school. He would prod for answers and details, but worse than in school, the correct answer did not stay the same for the same question. Who made the fort? We did. What do you mean We? Shurley and Winthrop, and me and Dolores. I don't want those Lynch kids over here every night! The Lynches had lived next door to us forever, we all played together all of the time. Except if we were mad at each other or had gotten into specific trouble that called for separation for a short and specified time. Which was not the case at the moment. It did not matter. Don't ask why. Don't even look like a smart aleck, the first syllable sound could be slapped into your caught-off-guard expression. Some drunk nights my question was angrily answered. Why didn't I wait on the side of caution? Why would I sometime ask why? Or why not? Why? (But tonight I did not say why out loud.) Tonight, we had exhausted ourselves in the snow, I was too tired to keep perfect time to the rhythm of his tension, I just felt like finishing my spelling.

Pay attention. Get through the meal. Do homework. Holding my breath, listen into the air for a clue. Daddy warns: No noise, no fooling around giggling. When we are in bed what will happen downstairs?

I fall asleep immediately. Wait. That is not what I planned. I wanted to stay on guard, to listen. I am scared awake by the silence. I need to figure out what it is, I don't hear any voices, I don't know how long I've been asleep. Feels late. What?

The sound of Daddy's shovel drags cross the cement floor, he always carefully stokes the furnace last thing at night. Banking it so it won't die out during the night and the whole family will sleep sound and warm. Still scared, half asleep, straining to hear their voices, I have to make everything okay. I hold my body so rigid I feel as if I have lifted off my mattress, listening. I cannot make out words, only tone. Their voices calm, ready to come upstairs to their bed. The temperature dropped, the damper was turned down so the draft pushed much less heat through than in the daytime.

I go to the warm kitchen to dress inside my blanket cocoon. All of our voices work back and forth perfectly normal the morning after Daddy was drunk, as if there wasn't anything to say or as if it didn't happen, as if it wasn't ever going to happen again. At breakfast all conversation was about weather. Is there much more snow? What is the temperature? Did the fort get buried?

When I was little, some nights we would listen to Mother sing and play the piano. My father would play the mandolin and try to sing too. How did they know all those songs that no one had ever heard of? We sang because we were having a good time. Camp songs, school songs, work songs, lullabies, hymns, heroic slave signals: Follow The Drinking Gourd.

How could a brutal evening be followed by a bright day with no explanation? No conversation of regret, or promise. Yet, when I think the word childhood the immediate is a flood of complex games. Play we structured and added to, to last for a week. And when my mother called time to come in, or my father came home drunk and embarrassing, the game was not put to an end. We had an unspoken to-be-continued that let us pick up and go on the following day.

IX

When I was 28 I married a man who was an orphan. Robert's father died when Robert was 8. His mother was hospitalized most of his life and died while he was in his teens. Robert told how his Grandpa Buck had him put into a foster home when he started cutting school. Robert grew up in a series of foster homes that saved him from truancy, stealing, and whatever would have come next. He ran away from several and finally was placed with a family who cared about this lonesome boy. He was not like other little boys. He wanted to read, all of the time, alone. These foster parents loved him and let him.

For all the time I knew Robert, no matter how I prodded, he always declared, I don't remember playing, I really never was a kid. Except, a single memory of his grandfather, Buck, his mother's father, placing little Robert astraddle his foot and singing three words, Splink, Splank, Splunk, Splink, Splink, Splunk, Splank.

Reaching back into our families we named our first son Robert. We named our second son for two grandfathers Daniel (maternal Daniel Diggs) and Buchanan (pronounced BUCK anan) for this man who played a game with small Robert Lee. A version of Ride-a-Cock-Horse-to-Banbury-Cross-to-See what my father played with me.

All of our children were in their teens when I said, Robert, you have to leave. I was in so much sad pain I knew I would be less lonely with him out of my every day. Robert was home every day after work. He was there on weekends. He was in the house but just vaguely a part of the household. I was sure that I could feel better with Robert out of reach since he would not (could not?) hold me. My husband took a small apartment not far from our house; we were separated for nine years but he was back home to cook every holiday. Robbie, Martha, Tisha and Dan went to his apartment every week without formal schedule; they rode their bikes or took the bus.

Once apart, Robert and I never discussed this separation. As if it did not exist we made no plans, we just lived in different homes. Neither of us asked for a divorce. Still if I accidentally ran into Robert there was the rush of first-glance reaction that always left me smiling surprised. What an attractive man?

Robert retired from the Cleveland school board when we had been separated eight or nine years. And out of nowhere we started seeing each other. Not frequently, but we were suddenly going to a movie or having dinner, checking out a special museum exhibit. Both going back to our separate homes as if this new behavior was normal. He had said, I am going to Germany for research, next spring, wanna-come. Oh? Well, yeah, sure. I answered without a pause as if casually agreeing, yes a matinee movie at the local suburban mall would be fine.

The two of us were at St. Luke's Hospital very early one morning, 6 a.m. We were nervous, not worried, a small nervousness since tests always mean results. He felt healthy, we were going abroad in the spring. Robert was working on another book on Black Literature, he would meet people he had been corresponding with, continue research and we both would play tourists. His German friends said it was the perfect time of the year. And we could see my friend Hester. Hester and I had been organizers at Senior Citizens' Coalition for years, now she lived in Munich.

I parked the car, Robert and I walked across the lot, into the hospital lobby, entered the intake cubby to register him for an outpatient surgical test, sure he'd be back at his apartment in the afternoon. The doctor had explained it all to us. I waited somewhat longer than we had been told but I waited without being frightened. His doctor took me to a semi-dark room to show the screened picture of Robert's blood vessels thinner than fine nylon thread and announced they would keep him to do a triple-bypass heart surgery. Robert insisted he had to go home and think it over, they said impossible, we are scheduling you for Friday.

A surgeon we did not even know chuckled, with that much damage, I don't know how you've been walking around. Robert's young cardiologist, Anne Mostow, held Robert's hand.

We had three full days to talk before his surgery, and we did not talk. We looked at crows and some sparrows on the parking lot outside his room. We drew a dead silence around us, with me keeping what I would, what I could-should say all tucked tight inside of my head. That is the way it had usually been, vague contact between us. Once in awhile, in the thirty-two years that we knew each other we would try, and fail, to speak what there was to say. We could say aloud that we loved each other, beyond that, not much.

Robert, a Black History scholar and a librarian, wore a trim beard to go with Burberry coat, tweed cap, soft leather gloves as uniform. His gray hair, thinning quite a bit at age 67, was already gray years before I first met him at Karamu House Theater, both of us first-time backstage volunteers. He was doing sound, I did props for a riotous production of Eugene Labiche's nineteenth-century farce, The Italian Straw Hat. Robert was reading a book throughout each act of the performance and still kept track of his sound cues. I was to learn that an open book in his lap was like part of his body. Robert never went anywhere without a book, he took his book in hand when he went to browse bookstores.

I loved listening to Robert backstage at Karamu, he could cite chapter and verse on one million things that I knew nothing about. One million things I knew something about, but had forgotten the details. Or the source. Married to Robert I did not have to look up anything that I had not learned or anything that had slipped my mind: Robert, Who was....? When was the....? Where did they....? What was that called? Just like that, he would have the short or detailed answer. That part of life with Robert was thrilling. In the hospital room, as I watched his body deep in coma, it was easy to remember what I missed. His answers and his ratatouille. I don't cook. Robert cooked. God, he made my life so easy, in some ways.

Robert, bird-watcher, had binoculars and lots of bird books. He could have named any strange bird for me, but nothing exotic flew near the hospital. I can correctly identify Big Black Crows. Nine crows stayed soaring outside the window. I have always liked crows, they're so big, so black, and raucous, they seem to be in charge.

The crows circled each day. Robert died caught in a 48-hour coma, eight days after we walked through St. Luke's glass lobby door.

We gave Robert this exquisite memorial, filling a beautiful small, red-carpeted amphitheatre at Cleveland State University, the Kiva. The service opened with a recording of Paul Robeson singing work songs. After family and lots of friends told what they remembered, we closed with Robeson's voice a cappella in gospel.

I wandered around wondering what to do with Robert's death. I had not been to work for a month. I was called to a board meeting and let them talk of paying my assistant, (and not me) with the little money they had left. It had been decided, no one warned me, I was not asked. Or told. No one mentioned ten years, hour-by-hour struggle to keep the organization alive. How could our work together have anything to do with the afternoon's conversation? It didn't matter. I could not do it any longer: Fight for my job, the organization, these old people, create an enthusiasm for money, mine or the organization's.

I slipped quietly from the room, I walked into the hall and wailed. Some of the board members came out. What's the matter, they asked, with Joan? Distancing me to third person. (I stay outside of the question, do not answer.) They confer to their own sure conclusion my crying was for my husband. After all it was only one month ago he died. Standing on the mezzanine of the Colonial Arcade I knew that if I had caught my breath, quelled my sobs to answer, I could not have said why I was crying. I remember wishing: Let my knees give way. I can sink to, no right straight through, the floor of this tired old building. What is directly below us? I couldn't remember what was below. What office, what store? And below the basement? Below this building is there a basement dug into the ground? Please, let my knees give way, please. These three old women are not strong enough to quickly catch me. There's the element of surprise! I disappear.

Two months later, my sister Tish called from Syracuse. Come, Mother is in the hospital. Maybe dying. Our mother died February 10, one day after her ninetieth birthday. At her senior citizens' center her friends said, Mrs. Harris was doing fine last week in crafts, I swear she could have taught the class herself.

Three deaths within five months was too much. Robert died without warning in the midst of incomplete plans. Giving sixty to eighty passionate hours a week to The Coalition had been my life for ten years and working came to an abrupt, pathetic end. My mother died at ninety. I was sixty years old (yet felt angrily orphaned), bewildered, completely abandoned and so tired. It makes perfect sense the amnesia could step forward into all that undefended space.

At my huge kitchen window, fragile tea cup in hand, small tidy yard in view, I felt a breeze blow, gently letting me watch a crucial answer float down. I could not move, no need to run.   Calm.   As if someplace I had always known.

I don't know how long I stood at my window, but the tea had cooled when I put the cup down.

That was the quiet beginning, but finding the amnesia lying there, exposed, left me in a state of shock. I remember what came next: terrorizing flashbacks. But How often How long How many? The months? years? meld into a space without numbers. Unyielding panic nighttime or daytime and my imperative still,

Don't Tell. Stuff it down to be examined later in darkness when I could allow memory and realization to ease out all of the jagged pieces.

Alone with the amnesia revealed, and telling no one, terror swallowed me. But I kept the reeling hidden. I went out, moved through my days: feeding my big, black cat, Nelson Mandela, nodding to neighbors, mowing the lawn. No one mentioned they saw me suffering, but inside I was frantically crazed. At some point in despair I finally called the Cleveland Rape Crisis Center. They held Incest Survivor Support Groups, and I telephoned, forcing myself to beg for entrance in modulated tone. I was afraid that if the receptionist heard a hint of my feeling of insanity, they would deem me too dangerous to come. If I did not get into their group my shrieking would burst and never stop. When they let me register, I felt as if I had fooled them. I went, the group was safe. Those women knew what I knew. They understood hiding horror and feeling crazy within what we survive. I was not alone.

Why didn't I realize? Why didn't I notice? How come no one told me? Made me look or listen? Why didn't someone tell and take care of me?

Amnesia, uncovered, is so stunning. This is how it must be when a mute (not deaf, just unable to speak) has something horrible to tell.

Three months after Robert died, all four of my children were home for the holidays. Everything was the same. The ceiling-touching tree that Robert could shop for but not carry in because he was allergic to pine tree sap. (He'd break out in long red welts all over his skin.) The tree was propped straight in the old painted metal tree stand that our neighbor Mrs. Clemmons had given years ago, I see you have four babies, I know they love Christmas, could you use this, I hate to throw it away. We were still using it and those babies were full-grown.

The aluminum-foil temporary star, that I had made for our first Christmas, long before we had any kids, was unpacked. Each year we take it out and smooth added foil over the brown carton ridges to cover any spots that had broken through. I do not remember whose turn it was to place the star on top of the tree.

I had to cook dinner, without Robert. We ate it without him there. The next day, before the children scattered across the country, I announced with noble selfless flourish that they had my permission to not all come home for Christmas the following year. They were grown, had lives to tend, and their own traditions to start. It was good to have had all of these years. We'll work out a schedule that brings us all here to Christmas celebration, every few years. What my heart wanted to say was, Let's go back! Come home for a week before Christmas. Stay another week until New Year's. All that business about your own Christmas tradition is a fake, I didn't really mean it. I don't want to be without you.

By February my mother was dead. I was not working but I was still so tired (unless retired means tired all over again). My mother had left me forever. The year had me barely hanging on, careening night after night into childhood horror. Awake because I could not sleep. Without sleep because I dared not close my eyes. Assaulted again and again by vivid flashbacks I could not stop. Shrieking within flashbacks so graphic I could not escape until they finished with me. And when they were done, I was alone, and still not protected from another and another. And another? Spending too many days and nights barely breathing.

The following year, just before Christmas, I felt a brand new awful flashback trying to close in. I tried to keep busy making a first Christmas when my four children (and Robert) would not be there. I wrote lists and schedules, I sewed, I cleaned. I made gifts.
Still there it hangs: My mother knew. Push past. Flail through it. Substitute an always known memory: I would wake at night and slowly realize that my mother was there. Across the room, sitting by the window, looking out, not at me. Maybe I called her name, Mother? the first time I saw her there in the night. But after the first time's question I only woke to watch her. We pretended that we never knew that I was awake and watching, that she was in my room. I would try so hard to stay awake, to keep my eyes

on her, but sleep would happen without my knowing it. I would be quietly awake watching her gaze out of the window, a blanket across her shoulders as if she would be there for a long while. All night. Suddenly, I would be asleep. Next it was morning. The chair was empty. Sometimes her blanket was still there. I think that she was standing guard. I think that I needed to watch her keeping me safe. And I did not want anything bad to happen to my mother. But, I never stayed awake longer than she did.

I still sit up at night. Or get up to walk around my house in the middle of the night. Mother used to say, I get some of my best work done at night, I have some of my best ideas. I know she always used to wander through the house at night. Watching. Waiting. Thinking. Taking care?

X

When I was little, the bustle would start weeks before every Christmas. All of the Sunday School classrooms became production arenas, the Sunday School superintendent and Ladies' Mission Society swung into high gear, each child had homework from church school, all of the mothers and a few fathers were besieged to sew, build and coach. Then once Thanksgiving was over, the whole AME Zion Church building began to sway with the rhythm of Sunday School pageant preparation.

I sat quiet and just waited for Sophronia Bennet's mother, our Sunday School class teacher, to look us over, judge the script and choose. She would glance down to scan the full page monologue then look at me, ask my opinion, Joan, do you think, you can do this one? So that I could answer, Yes, I think I can.

We never were better behaved than in the month of December. We took you-better-watch-out, Santa-Claus-is-coming as serious threat even when we did not necessarily believe in Santa. We tried harder to be good but we got giddy. Word could swiftly be passed directly to your mother if church elders had us suddenly tangled around their ankles when I was chasing Mary Elizabeth playing tag in the church basement. In spite of the fact I had promised Miss Bennett I would wait quietly for my cousin, it just sorta happened we both really, really had to use the bathroom at the same time. Depending on who caught us, we might get a direct scolding and warning or much worse, we could be taken to interrupt my mother and the other mothers as they laid out costume design. Joan, you know better than run inside the church. Apologize and go back to your room. And I did. We did, both of us, Mary Elizabeth and me.

  I always had Mary Elizabeth as my close friend. We didn't live close enough to go to school together, but we went to the same church, which meant the same picnics and summer Vacation Bible School, same excursions, holiday programs with all of the preliminary plans and rehearsals.

  I have four children, two boys, two girls, just like in my growing up family, but my kids did not have any hometown cousins to grow up with day to day. I now live in the house that my kids grew up in from toddlers until they left. Most of the families on my block have lived here thirty years or longer. Within the last few years we have had some senior citizens move on and some young families move in. A family, mother, father, adolescent son and daughter, has just moved into the Walkers' old house across the street. The street does not know them yet, but zealously excluding old Mrs. Cotton disdainfully refers to them as Those Jehovah's Witness People. How does she find out that kind of stuff? Their name is Crumb.

Bald, pale yellow, Mr. Crumb and his young brown son in an old man's tan suit got into their car, each carrying a gusseted leather briefcase. The fourteen-year old son almost looked bald too, he carried himself so prim beside his father.

I watched the Crumbs and I thought of my father.

My father never spoke of religion or God or church. I had decided early on that that long row of loud deacons, importantly up there in the front pew, could not possibly have small kids who played outside or went to school. Fathers stayed home. Mothers and children went to Sunday School and sermons.

My father's mother was Jehovah's Witness. I never thought of him as that! He never went to church or Kingdom Halls. It was watching Crumb and son that made me think of him. I remember someone (his mother or mine?) telling me that his mother was so special a Witness, that she had earned the rank of those that would be the first to enter the Kingdom on the Great Getting-up Morning. I used to daydream with wonder because they said this, even after she was dead, and that had to mean that before all the millions and billions of people who were still alive, the really great good people who were already in Heaven would be gathered up, and God would tell Letitia Harris, Come, be first in line. Wow. Chosen to be the first in line, no matter what, no matter if you happen to have died already or something. You still get touched, picked, and it was a covenant, a promise that wouldn't be forgotten or overlooked in all the excitement or in all of the people of the world, living or dead!!!!!

As I watched the Crumbs from my house on Kempton, I wondered if my father, as a small boy, walked with his mother and knocked on neighbors' doors to bring them the light.

Grandmother Harris with her sons, Falstaff and Mordecai.

From Shurley on, we each recited the same Sunday School poem when we were only two or three years old. The words were church tradition, but each Harris kid was celebrated with individual family story of our adorable small singsong sway.

What are you looking at me so funny for?
I didn't come to stay
I just came to wish you
A Merry Christmas Day
(Curtsey: front, side, dip, with skirt daintily furled)

Remember how Joan curtseyed into the wings when she had gotten all turned around? Circling to scratch her shoulder, pick at her sash, pull at socks and hair ribbons all at the same time. And remember Winthrop recited fine, bowed proudly, then seemed to want to stay on stage for the rest of his life. He had to be taken by the hand and led gently, firmly from the applause.

We stayed a part of Sunday School well into our teens. I liked memorizing very long poems. While she cooked or while we cleaned house together, my mother recited poetry in the same way that other mothers sing to their children. She knew so many poets (white and black), classic, literary or comic vaudeville. She and Aunt Belle were local stars when they were teenagers in the small town of Auburn and had taken their young ladies' act to church functions, school programs and afternoon ladies' teas. So, my mother was our coach, and we were good. We carefully worked our way through exquisite traditional Negro poetry: Paul Laurence Dunbar. Pages-long The Creation by James Weldon Johnson. Eloquent essays from W.E.B. DuBois' *The Souls Of Black Folk*. He used Black proudly in the days when we all were proudly colored, and for most colored, black was a pejorative. Bitter, precise Countee Cullen, ... To make a poet black, And bid him sing.

Mother said, forget the end of the line and read the whole meaning. That is really how the poet wrote it. I would read. She would listen. Then ask me what I thought I said. If it happened to rhyme, Mother said that didn't matter it still was about the whole idea. Before I started to memorize the stanzas she would listen to me read it over and over finding the story. Today when I read classics, like James Weldon Johnson's gospel sermon, The Creation, I hear my mother's voice and mine in soft duet:

> And God stepped out on space,
> And He looked around and said:
> I'm lonely
> I'll make me a world.

The A.M.E. Zion Church is small, gray-stoned short-spired. The building is still solidly there and not in use now. My sister Tish has a doable daydream of buying it to use as a museum for her vast collection of Black antique books, slave history and memorabilia

It was almost always only women working hard on preparation, but fathers showed up the night of performance. The pews were completely filled. Pageant sounded grand and appropriate for the time, love, and community effort, but the actual evening was probably closer to Major Bowes' Amateur Hour. There was a gentle, pleased announcer naming child after child, and who they belonged to. All standing to sing solo or in duet, recite a poem with vigorous declamation or shy mumble. The finale was children costumed as manger animals. The final encore bows would bring down the house. Every participant, still inwardly flying, would retire to the church basement for cookies and huge punch bowls of juice with gingerale and floating ice cream added for the occasion. My father would be proudly sitting in the audience to see us perform. Then he would join the crowd of worshipers as they slowly flowed down into the basement where they could hold napkin, cookie, and punch in their hands. Every once in a while a grownup would mildly call, you children be careful, now. Perhaps there would be a firm adult hand to block a dangerous headlong plunge. No one grew truly impatient enough to stop our whirling games. You're It! and I Gotcha Back! all around, and in and out of knees and elbows of the satisfied congregation.

Mother gave Shurley the name Nervous de Purvis. He really was excitable. Always on the sharp edge of discovery. I can hear his voice raised in amazement, exactly the same at seventeen and at seventy, Come on look jeez look! Wow, See that! Jeez, Comehearsee: the colored bright underbelly of a snake; a huge intricately twisted fungus that attached to our tree overnight; the choice of textures Romare Bearden wedged together for his Black Manhattan Collage; Shurley's insect-sized toads all singing to each other; his own blueprints from art class and from work. Shurley graduated from Syracuse University's School of Fine Arts, just like our father, and then he quickly became head of the design department at SYROCO, Syracuse Ornamental Company.

Even after he retired he continued to work, consulting or creating his own projects. When he died, at 73, he left unfinished a contract for a birdhouse to be distributed through a national catalogue. There I stood glowing in the midst of the same intense teaching, as he let me handle the design sheets and the cardstock prototype with his running lecture proving the simple assembly and spare beautiful design. Shurley was nine years older than me and five years older than Winthrop. He probably enjoyed being big brother. I'm not sure which came first, our adoration or his steady stream of information, ideas and projects that kept us running and begging to keep up with him. Bragging to all of the other kids, Can't ya Shurley? Don't ya, Shurley? He was outstanding. Brilliant, curious, clever, funny. When he came home from a hike with a jar full of frogs, within a few hours he would have examined them and pored through our encyclopedia so all of us kids, siblings and friends, learned this frog's habitat, habits and lifespan.

There was a small corner porch at the back entrance of our house. Although Mother used it to hang a few pieces of laundry and I'd play house on the steps, it was for the most part Shurley's place. He kept frogs, snakes, toads, guinea pigs, praying mantis, ants, earthworms, bright-marked spiders and a couple different times a gigantic snapping turtle. Shurley allowed us to catch the bugs for his menagerie. All size grasshoppers lived in the tall grass of the Old Lot; we patiently waited for them to settle on a weed leaf so we could cup them in our hand and transfer them to the bug jar. We learned to trap flies gently against the screen door with our palm. Even when we figured out that we were doing him a favor instead of vice versa we still loved to catch live food.

Shurley made places for all of his captured things, a glass jar with holes punched in the top with the ice pick, or netting stretched across with a huge rubber band was temporary housing or just a place to keep food alive. He designed terrariums with mini-ponds surrounded by plants, or split-level observation boxes made of wire screening and wood framed with a hinged top.

My brother Shurley rushed yelling at every new thing, his creation or nature's. Wow, look how it works. Isn't that great?

At the top of his lungs, old Nervous de Purvis could be heard a block away. Ma. Ma. Look what we got. My mother rushed out to hear his announcement. Shurley, Winthrop, Roy Crawford and Glenn Fikes had been gone since 5:30 in the morning. She could see he was holding high a bulging, orange-net, ten-pound onion sack. His plans bubbling out as they ran. We caught a hundred, we're gonna make belts and sell them! he screamed. She yelled back at the wriggling sack, you take those snakes back where you found them. Right Now!

Only a few weeks before, Mother had come out on the porch barefoot late one night, Shurley's pet snake had escaped. In the dark Mother stepped on it, she almost died, and the snake really did. Lord knows how many of the sackful would slither free before they were skinned.

He really thought she would be delighted, he had finally forgiven her for the snake killing. He expected she'd be as thrilled as he was, people paid good money for snakeskin belts, they had found some beauties and Mother knew how to make incredible finds at The Rum. Shurley, Roy, Glenn and Winthrop would do all the work of the belt itself and Mother could match them up with buckles from belts she could find really cheap. Good craftsmanship, logical business sense. Shurley was bewildered. Mother unrelenting.

We are telling the bag of snakes story to a fourth generation. It will be told to our kids who never knew him.

You have to be able to raise your voice to a high Nervous de Purvis shriek, for true color. Jeez, look at this. Come and see.

We called my cousin: Little Lawrence.

My uncle was: Big Lawrence (although he was a slender man, average height). When they called my brother Winthrop little, he did not like it. Winthrop was not a junior and Winthrop wanted to be bigger. He came home from kindergarten to announce that he was the biggest child in his class. My mother said she smiled but did not question Win or talk about it much again even when the class picture came home with all of the children perched in four rows, small Winthrop front row end, to balance the class picture, tall to tiny. Winthrop seated cross-legged and attentive. None of us are anywhere near tall.

Gordon Bakery delivered fresh-baked goods to Mr. Johnson's and Mrs. Arkin's and stores all over town. You could go to the side door and buy a number ten size brown paper grocery sack piled high to barely closing with leftover half-moon cookies and kueghlie and cream puffs with real whipped cream and filled chocolate eclairs. Only ten cents for the whole bag because they were day-old brought back from the retail stores. When Winthrop was so sick that most of the time he slept alone all during the day in the boys' bedroom when all the other kids were in school and his bedroom shades were pulled down to the windowsill so the light would not hurt his eyes, I was allowed to go all the way down Raynor cross Adams down Almond past the big Sears Roebuck near Rothschild Drugstore all by myself and bring the bag to Winthrop's bedside where he could have first pick as we discovered how lucky we had been today.

In school we memorized Robert Louis Stevenson's poem When I Was Sick And Lay Abed, of counterpanes and toy soldiers. Win helped me practice so I could recite it perfect in class. He missed school and they missed him. Grandma Diggs stayed for long visits the year Winthrop was sick. Grandmother used to say, little-boy-so-lonely, wistfully under her breath, not talking to Winthrop or anyone. It was a one-line poem to go with her gaze, repeated throughout her stay.

It was mid-afternoon. My friend Marilyn Cox had come over just after lunch. We hunkered low over tiny toy cars, racing the highway we'd etched into the gravel drive, probably headed to Hollywood. Playing right near the steps of my side porch. I hear my mother's voice. She starts calling my name from inside the house, before she even comes through the kitchen door and down the porch steps. My mother held my shoulders with firm hands and looked straight in my eyes as she spoke. Marilyn listened and went home. I think. I stood close, still, already out of breath from running the errand I was to start.
Don't wait your turn. Don't wait my turn.
Say excuse me. Excuse me, please, Mrs. Arkin, call an ambulance.
Winthrop Harris, 616 Renwick Avenue. And run! Renwick Avenue Rheumatic Heart Renwick Avenue Rheumatic Heart Renwick Avenue Rheumatic Heart ... Be sure and say rheumatic heart so they'll know he's been

sick. I did not leave the store until after Mrs. Arkin went to the phone. I didn't cry until I was running back home. I was eight years old, so my brother Winthrop was only thirteen.

Winthrop was just enough older to not be jealous of her arrival. We always called Tish Winthrop's baby. He liked taking care of her and could still do some of the slow quiet things that babies need even after he got sick.

He had missed a whole year of school, and he loved school. My father always said that if Winthrop had gotten to grow up he would have been a mathematician.

When he got sick, I held the small brown bottle, while my mother gave Winthrop a teaspoon of Cod Liver Oil. If Winthrop tried to rest, I tiptoed quietly and whispered whenever I was reminded. Dr. Coleman said over-ripe bananas were easily digested and filled with potassium and vitamins that would be good for Winthrop. The black-skinned bananas looked rotten, so soft they were almost liquid. These prescribed slimy bananas were nasty but I peeled them, convinced I was keeping my brother alive.

When I got back from Mrs. Arkin's, Mother had sent a neighbor for Aunt Belle. I had to Sit on the Steps and Watch for the Ambulance! It came without sirens and crunched its wheels through our gravel miniature park. Even after the ambulance came they wouldn't let me come in. I sat out of the way, on the side porch steps, and listened to all of the noise inside of my house.

Dr. Madison came, so did Grandmother and Aunt Belle. The ambulance left and did not take my brother. They'd been there a long time. It was already dark and we still couldn't find Daddy. I heard everyone talking about looking everywhere. Grandmother kept checking to report Winthrop's little cheeks and hands are still warm. Shurley's face was buried inside his folded arms at the dining room table. Mother sat beside the kitchen table, without the overhead light. My father came in from drinking and did not know what had happened. I held my breath. Hiding. Quiet. Then I eased back on my heels, in the corner of the room, to look up and watch my small grandmother wiping a big soft damp bath towel at the tears on Daddy's face. They stood in the dining room threshold, framed in slow motion. Then he went toward the bottom of the stairs, with his fedora and top coat still on. He hadn't yet gone to see Winthrop, hadn't touched his hand to his hat when he started up the steps.

They all forgot I was there from the time I'd run to Mrs. Arkin's for the ambulance. I wanted them to say they were proud that I'd run really fast. I wanted them to ask if I was hungry. I wanted them to notice I was up way past my bedtime, and I wanted them to say I could stay up the rest of the night.

My grandmother came, wiped over my hands and face with a wet terry washcloth, took my hand in hers, led the way up the stairs to make me peer at Winthrop dead, on his bed, in his own neatened bedroom. His cheeks looked warm, I did not dare to touch them. His hair had been combed and brushed, his pillow puffed up full. And he was tucked in so nice and cozy I was sure my brother Winthrop wanted to turn to see me. We all were absolutely quiet for a long long while. By the time we came back downstairs my father had started making terrible hard sounds to go with his tears. They did not take my brother out of the house until very late that night and when they took him on a gurney Winthrop's face was covered with a blanket and he was going to the Garfield Brothers Mortuary.

Joan, age 7

XI

Alone in my house I say loud aloud:
 Mother   (sigh),   Mother.

This happens often, it comes without thinking. It darts into the air I hear and I don't really know it is a familiar English title. I may have said it several times before I recognize it as a proper noun, before I realize I am calling her and she is dead, and I am 69, and what do I want her to come to me for? What do I want her to say?

I repeat

Mother   oh   Mother

I grew up thinking that I was my mother's favorite. I mean all the way to being an old adult, when Mother and Tish lived in Tish's two-family house in Syracuse, and I had been away for forty years. And then, as I watched and knew how much she gave and shared with my sister, it seemed like a silly kid's joke. I still appreciate the comfort of that childhood misconception. What if our mother had a trick to make each of us feel most loved?

When Mother had had several mild strokes it seemed the doctors were doing all the wrong things. My little sister read the PDR (Physician's Desk Reference), discovered a prescription's terrible emotional side effects on older adults and redirected her treatment. I asked Tish: Tish, how did you do it? How did you balance job, worry, groceries and still watch Mom's medicine and appetite, her worry about bills and household? How did you hold Mother's brittle body as she screamed and pounded you as her imagined attackers, then convince Mother to remember and laugh at her terrorizing hallucinations the moment they ended? Tish answered, Oh. I always thought of us as two single mothers helping each other out.

Mother and Junior, Gianna and Tish together in a two-family house. My sister always presents bright simple fact. She hands me these small gifts of gentle obvious. I thank her, because I might never have figured it out by myself. So after Tish's divorce, Mother watched four-year-old Gianna while my sister went to work. And when Gianna was grown, Tish brought Mother amazingly all the way through a difficult recuperation. After Mother died, Tish continued to take care of Junior until he died two years later.

They used to say Mongoloids don't live much past adolescence, but he grew to be an old man and did not look his age. Back then they said Mongoloid or Mongolian Idiot instead of

Down Syndrome. He was my baby as Tish had been Win's. A safe ownership since we each had a sibling between. He was fat and brown and had lots of hair, he looked exactly as he should, at first. He was beautiful. I happily held him. Tish, as displaced baby-of-the-family, tried to draw Grandma into whispered conspiracy.

Let's throw him in the garbage, Grandma.

Mother was in bed for almost two weeks. She used the same bedpan that Winthrop had used, Grandmother in and out of the room emptying it. Pulled window shades darkened my mother's bedroom all through the day, there wasn't enough sunlight for me to see how she was doing. Mother flat on her back barely moving. Tired? Sick? Tish and I warned to keep all of our noise outside in the yard. The house was quiet. Even the baby didn't cry very loud.

He was born a year after Winthrop died. A fifth child, third son. And they named him Falstaff Lionel Harris Junior. Mother worried about his short fingers from the beginning. Grandma marveled at each thing he learned and remembered, See there, that boy's as smart as can be! He couldn't talk. He didn't sit steadily, could not pull himself up to stand. I carried him around on my hip, he was pretty and he was mine. Daddy would prop him against the couch for hours and coax, beg him forward. Junior did not take his first steps until he was three years old. Everyone called him the baby, and used Baby as his name until he was nine. It took a long time for me to admit he was different. Grandma never minded.

I sit up at night because I am afraid to go to bed. I do not talk much about the sitting up part. I do sometimes mention, when asked, four hours of sleep is all I need, I've always functioned fine on four hours. I think I wake up before I allow myself dreams. I rarely dream. I dare not dream. That would be unmonitored images. My night dreams were stamped out so there would be no danger of questions raised by anyone, not even by me. All sound and pictures destroyed; after all, dreams are only images. Imaging while we are asleep. When I was very small I dreamed, I think. Dreaming must have ended sometime after the touching started with my father's urgent threat: Don't tell.

Never sleeping through the night, like my mother, who would wake to walk and keep watch through the night, I still am on guard against the accidental nightmare cantering into my sleep screaming a question that might demand an answer. It feels like I thought I had to protect my mother or he would do something horrible like this to her. It feels as if I thought I had to protect him, that I thought he was in pain. Felt like I was the secret head of the family, in charge of keeping all of us safe.

When I watched Mother sit in my bedroom scared and angry on nights Daddy had been rampaging drunk, we were all safe as long as he slept. If he found her in there when he woke before morning, he had calmed down, or forgotten, or slept it off enough, to stumble away if she shushed and chased him, I am not coming in there Falstaff! Go away, you'll wake up the kids.

How come when we were old, Tish remembered my mother once told her, you know Joan provoked a lot of that stuff, (they'd been talking about the fights). As if the fights were only with me! As if he did not beat her, and beat Shurley. As if we never had to call the police. As if the police did not come sometimes when she was the one being slapped and punched.

So sometimes even all those years later, Mother thought she could have stopped the fights if she had kept her mouth shut. She still thought, If Joan had not answered back. If Joan had not run and told Shurley to come help, hurry.

How could she think even then, when he was dead, that the fights were my fauult? Or her fault?

I must have been around seven or eight when I found what looked like pus on my belly. I got undressed to get into the tub, there was some pus on my stomach, right near my belly button. It looked like pus, it was white and starting to dry, when I rubbed my finger across it was slightly sticky. I could not remember cutting myself. How curious. That's odd. I studied it bewildered.

This was a very different discovery from finding a healing wound. When I used to spend time picking a scab on my elbow or knee that was worthwhile. It was pass-time, I could spend a slow half hour doing that. And I had developed it into a science, pick carefully around the edge to make sure the scab was ripe, ready to be lifted with a little extra help from my fingernail. Pull, but not too quickly, work my way to the core. If it was time, it would lift with no bleeding center, not too soon to need a new growth of scabbing. I would ease it up and out of the white dimple of uncolored skin, then spread it across my fingertip pleased that I managed to lift it intact. And the cut would continue to heal. With a scab I remembered the fall or scrape. Always. Why was pus coming out of my belly button? How peculiar, especially since it didn't hurt, even poking there was no sore evidence of a wound.

But I didn't tell my mother.

It washed away with soap and water on a washcloth. And it never hurt. Or bled. Or formed a scab to heal for exploring.

But there it was again. Dried and trailing a thin path down my stomach. What? and again. Now what. Finally, I lifted up my dress and showed my mother: It doesn't hurt. And I didn't fall. Or pick at it?

I always had secretly worried about being the only one in the family with a belly button that poked straight out instead of the way a normal navel folded inside its own small pocket of skin. Now what had I done?

Mother rested her hands on my shoulders to turn me toward the light. She bent down to peer closely without touching it. Muttered hummmm, and didn't know what to make of it either, but told me to go take a bath, we would let Dr. Madison take a look. (No one ever went to a doctor without a bath and clean underwear, no matter how high your temperature or deep your pain.) I liked going to see our sweet bumbling absent-minded family doctor. But I did not feel sick. Nothing hurt me. We told my father. My mother took me.

I climbed up on the examining table. I kept my panties and undershirt on, moved them down slightly and my undershirt up out of the way. Dr. Madison pulled the bright doctor's office light close so I could be examined. And there was nothing to see. So Dr. Madison told my mother he couldn't find anything wrong, even with prodding. We should come see him again if there was a problem.

My father was waiting worried in the living room for me and Mother to get home and tell him what the doctor said. We were all glad he said I was fine. I never found pus, wet or dry, on my stomach again.

Why didn't she guess that the pus on my belly was not pus? I did not know what semen was, but she had to have looked when she washed it off her own thighs. She had to have seen semen some time during the years they had been married at the time I was showing her what I thought was pus from my belly button.

I don't know what is worse; she thought I knew and was just showing it? She had suspected what he had done and could not figure out what to do? What would a woman do at a time before sex had even been invented? Sex was never considered a topic to be raised in any conversation. The word sex was not ever spoken. The marriage bed was to be endured in the dark and with eyes closed. A wife could celebrate their silver wedding anniversary without ever having looked at an adult penis. There is no answer. What would have happened if she had confronted him? He would act as if he did not know what she was saying. He would slap her hard across her mouth for even thinking something so disgusting. He would kill her? He would kill himself? I don't think killing was a real possibility. Ordinary people like us could not be murderers, back then.

    My mother kept going by keepin' keepin' on. With all that I know about back then, there is no way a family like us could say "semen." When I was twelve, Mother lowered her eyes and handed me a folded white linen napkin, put this between your legs she muttered. Back then that was the complete mother-daughter discussion when I started to bleed and had no idea why (and could not ask), did not know that it was supposed to happen to me again the following month. When I was surprised, Mother explained, this is called your monthly.

    So, where are your pins?

    My mother had the same two safety pins she used every month since she started menstruating. I didn't keep track of my large safety pins from the first month to the second. I used to teasingly torment Mother in retelling my first monthly by claiming she handed me a folded tablecloth to pin between my legs along with her terse explanation.

I used cloths attached to my underpants with safety pins until I asked to buy Kotex Pads when I finally figured out that this was the whispered secret that Bea, Evalyn and Ernestine had excluded me from because they had started first, therefore felt smugly more grown-up. In the school cloakroom they had whispered and seemingly plotted within earshot, Shhh, Joan doesn't know, and I didn't. There were so many things without names back then, and only some could I figure out on my own. Back then the rules said: Leave Much Unspoken. And I questioned.

The ..... had no name. And the ...... was my father? I had to save myself all by myself. Think how brilliant. Stay very very quiet and hide in place. Don't cry, don't scream, don't breathe, don't even try to whisper. If I moved or made a sound, more pain would find me.

There were times when my incest flashbacks were preceded by warning, the smell and taste of dread. There was one that came back again and again sometimes with warning, sometimes not. I have always been small and short. Then, I was tiny:

He holds his hand backward across my mouth, presses his fingers deep in my cheek and cuts off my breathing with his hard, strong palm, while his penis is inside me and his stomach pumps against my pubis faster and faster. He keeps his voice at whisper. My father's deep-throated threat and breathing is squeezeforced into my ear. The Words. The hot dark words are worst. This pain has nothing to do with my vagina. All of the pain above my waist is so sheer I cannot think, I do not know what is happening.   A person, gigantic. His thrust stretches against my heart, tears through to my throat, and my throat is scarred.

  It was discovering amnesia that overwhelmed and distressed me. Not the incest, not the rapist, not the pain. I hid inside of sadness in my house, and lost day after day in prolonged keening, weeks, months in agonizing remorse that I had not recognized the clues. How could I have not known, not paid attention? There were obvious signs all along. I sank deep, hating that my introspective self had danced all around and over. Skipped past disclosure. The drunken beatings I remembered but the rapes were left out of all those years as sister, wife, mother, caseworker, counselor, or friend.

  How could I have let this happen? How could I have been so stupid? So unstrong? To not have recognized the obvious presence of amnesia left me railing and crazed. It was as if forgetting was so terrible it made me worthless. The amnesia alone tortured me, there was no time for the specifics of what it held. Looking back, that feels like stage two. Mourning first, the amnesia second. Three: the incest flashbacks. It had come in stages. There was no way I could have physically survived attending to all three at once. My body could only withstand enormous pounding one attack at a time.

Quick succession, no let-up, no breather. Bam. Bam. Bam. Finally the engulfing grip of an incest flashback with heat, smell, sound and all the details of raw vision through squinched child-eyes. An incest flashback is unrelenting, inescapable, when you are inside one you know you can die.

During this time, I longed to speak with people who had some kind of history in my life. I wanted Robert. I thought if he were still here I could explain what had been wrong. If I started talking about this maybe he would talk too.

Robert read everything, knew everything; when Robert was here I'd ask, Robert, where did Shakespeare say ... first kill all of the lawyers? And Robert would pronounce, it was his fifth sonnet or maybe he'd say, Laertes speaking to Portia in the second scene of *The Merchant of Verona* after the ghost had filled the cauldron. And the full quote is, First kill all of the Philadelphia lawyers before the trial has even begun. Except Robert would say what was truly accurate. If Robert was here I'd have authoritative context and I would be attended as profound and appropriate.

If Robert were here I'd be eating his homemade chicken and rice stuff, maybe Thompson's Turkey or perhaps he'd make ratatouille. But he is dead and has been gone so long I'd have to take one of his million cookbooks off of my bookshelves and search to remember the ingredients of that lovely melodious word. Ratatouille.

If Robert were here we would be able to speak of how much has been lost. If Robert were here, and I had already told him I'd found the amnesia, when an incest flashback happened he might have been able to hold me until it had passed.

I needed to let Ilse, my best friend, know. Ilse and I met in the very first class of our freshman year at Syracuse University. From that 8:00 a.m. biology lab orientation we were friends for life. The plan was to grow into old ladies together and annoy our husbands and bore our children and grandchildren with same-old-same-old-stories. We used to sometimes cut class and go downtown. I would stand aside looking innocent as Ilse bought our movie tickets. At twenty, I easily passed for under twelve, but we dared not giggle until we got inside the theater. It all felt very adventurous. Two movies, newsreel, and cartoon with popcorn, plus hot dogs and root beer at Woolworth's 5 & 10 stand-up counter after. Then, since continuous-showing was standard at that time, we could go see a second double feature at the theater across the street. We saw the fairy tale romance, *The Red Shoes*, six times. We liked all the same parts in Jean Renoir's *The River*, sighed simultaneously as the lovely East-Indian actress calmly said, consent.

Our four years at Syracuse gave time for Ilse to become part of my family. We lived together in New York City after I finished graduate school. Ilse died when her son, Keith was in junior high, after multiple sclerosis had weakened her steadily, too quickly and too soon for her to go. Ilse knew all of my secrets. All of the secrets that I knew. And we could have cried together over finding out about the amnesia and incest. We would have carried it around and talked it to death, at my house, at her house, beside Seth's pond on The Vineyard.

Way back when no one mentioned the unmentionable, it was sometimes funny how little we knew. My mother laughed about her expectation of the male body shape when she got married, she had heard the slang word balls and girlfriends had told her the balls' general location. Though she planned to keep her eyes closed (through her entire married life?) sometime in the first few years she saw what did not look like two side-by-side baseballs. I never asked if she had expected the ovoid stitching and trade mark, or if she had expected them to be bright white. We were both laughing hysterically at this point of her story and I did not want to wet my pants before she finished the tale, anyway she had deduced that if there were balls, the penis (though she never used this word to me), the poojee-pahjee, would be shaped exactly like a baseball bat. This conversation did not take place until she was grandmother to my school-age children. But not in front of the kids.

When I was able to admit the amnesia I called my sister. I could not begin to talk over the phone, at first I only asked her to come to Cleveland to visit. She was working, there were meetings set that she could not get out of. I did not say: This is important. I called again, still sounding casual. I desperately wanted to see my sister but could not bring myself to go home. It felt as if Syracuse would not be safe even though my father had died thirty years ago. Mother was dead, she could not protect me. There was too much to tell by phone. On a third phone call, three or four weeks later, I whispered, Tish, please can you come see me? I cannot come to Syracuse with Mother not there anymore, and Daddy is.

My sister did not ask what I meant, she did not think I had lost mind. She came. We talked round the clock for a four-day weekend.

Tish Knew.

Tish tells me she clearly remembers an almost killing, terrible shrieks, screams, furniture tumbling, worse, different than ever before. She came out to see Shurley had knocked my father down and was still punching him, seething Don't you ever touch Joan again! She tells me but I cannot bring it up to recall. I was there, yet no matter how hard I try, I can't see that night's sequence and sound. Yet I could see it was a scene that makes perfect sense, it felt sure even without the lost image.

My sister tells me she asked did Daddy molest you? when we were adults. I do not remember her ever asking. She insists she asked several times over the years. Her questions came out of remembering that night I still don't remember, and several other incidents always troubled her. She remembered me being hysterical when he had opened the bathroom door once when we were in the tub. Tish tells me my dismissive reaction to her question later in our lives was always no. No, I don't remember, it was probably prepubescent privacy, body barely changing etc., etc., etc. I still don't remember either incident nor those conversations about them. But my sister came to Cleveland and stayed with me because she knew exactly what I meant when I called. What would I do without her? We talked drinking tea in my kitchen, and we talked stretched across the bed late into the night. We walked to the Cleveland Greenhouse to talk sheltered by gnarled trees in the dark Japanese garden. Sitting on the front porch steps it was the same as when we were children talking, we laughed, and talked some more.

  Talking to Tish made it all right to tell. I wrote a detailed long letter to Martha, Robbie, Tisha and Danny. My brother was back living in Syracuse, so Tish told Shurley as soon as she got there. She called me to say how much they cried together. Their tears were enough to wash away my father's ghost, and I needed to go tell Shurley thank you. He must have known he was adored, I hope he knew he was adored, I wanted to be sure to say out loud, thank you for everything. The cemetery ride; tips on how to shape the tiles on my drawing of the Chinese pagoda; letting me sometimes come with the big boys when you guys snuck onto the grounds of that mansion on the way to Thornden Park where we could sit on that huge metal manhole-cover-shaped thing that wound us round and round like spinning carousel. With you and Glenn and Roy running fast, pushing hard then jumping on to join the little kids. I was young enough to assume rich people built special toys for their rich kids, how was I to know it was to turn their cars in a tightly spaced driveway? Thank you for protecting me often and especially for trying to, on that night I can not remember. He didn't want to talk about that. Shurley cried, sobbed and wished I still did not know, he would not let us go there. We did talk of the day we almost got caught playing in the secluded driveway. Nine or ten kids all sizes and colors running, screaming, escaping, to laugh falling down once we were safe out-of-reach hidden on a green Thornden Park hill.

There in Syracuse he showed me what he was currently working on. At high Nervous de Purvis energy we looked at his beautiful birdhouse and went over the blueprint and contract for distribution and sale. We laughed while he planned, until Shurley wound down slumped in his overstuffed chair, talking slowly, his hand resting on a flat half-filled bottle of liquor lying on the floor. He told me he had terminal cancer. Six months later Shurley died.

My brother Shurley must have known at least two fathers. He was an only child until he was almost five years old. Shurley loved to draw from the time he was a little tiny kid, an artist just like his father. Shurley knew my mother and father when they must have been young, silly, successfully upwardly-mobile even though that phrase had not yet been coined. We have pictures of my father young and playing tennis; a snapshot of him swooping my giggling mother up into his arms; group photos of all the Diggs girls and their beaus, before everyone was married to become Daddy, Uncle Lawrence and Uncle Al. So, Shurley must have known so much more.

My mother used to say, "They'll never believe it!" She would often finish a description or story with, I am going to stop telling all the things I know or have seen, they'll never believe it. On the phone my sister and I are laughing. Tish tells about an afternoon the words they'll-never-believe were out of mother's mouth before Tish could close hers, as a pigeon swooped out of nowhere and took a piece of fresh crackerjack from her fingertips just as she was about to pop it in her mouth. A sunny day downtown, on Salina, our main street, lots of busy shoppers crowding by, and Tish did not have time to close her mouth before pigeon and mother had played their parts. They'll never believe me! Then they all laughed, loud and choking. I know as he tried to swallow the pigeon was giggling too,

XII

When I was little my mother, sister, brothers and I staked out the best downtown curb location for every hometown parade mounted. We were there a good hour before broad Salina Street filled with the first band. I need a parade, now. I think a gigantic parade would do. I love the brass and the cymbals. Uncurling bright serpentine paper, crowds cheering along the way. I want to see me, seated high in the back seat of a 1929 bright yellow Duesenberg convertible. Waving, smiling, laughing out loud.

My mother used to say, when she was little there was an early morning unofficial circus parade. Elephants, cages of lions, roustabouts and midgets unloading to set up the Big Tent. Her father, Daniel Diggs, would wake Evelyn, Pauline, Ed and Isabel at 4:00 a.m. Half asleep and completely excited in semi-dark they would go downtown by trolley to see this parade sans band, only the rhythm of plod and screamed orders. She said, and I believed, that the men walking alongside with long spike tipped sticks poked the elephants to keep them from peeing, in order to stop an elephant-size pee flood.

Mother packed her stories of olden days tightly in between everything we needed to carry with us; popcorn that we helped shake and bag, candies that were cheaper from the Five and Dime, sweaters if it was autumn, visors that we designed and crayoned if it was the Fourth of July. Then with the parade in progress the grinning clown/salesman skipped by, Ma, can I have a balloon? And my mother would pull the color of my choice from her bag, blow it up, and twist it at the end of one of the five thin reusable wooden dowels she had brought with us. The balloon was in my hand.

Back then, play took a stretched comforting time because of the details, the planning and the costumes. The dress-up supply (from The Rum, of course) was infinite. My days could be as ordinary housewife (apron that covered back and front of gingham-checked house dress) or society dam (a broad saucer-brim velvet hat held a piled helping of slim black fluttering feathers).

Though Shurley was almost ten years older than I was, Winthrop was in the middle between us. My brothers were close. Winthrop was enough younger to whisper late-night tales of Shurley's brilliance and bravery, Can't ya, Shurley? Din'cha, Shurley? Once in a while, Winthrop would join my pretend; small for his age he blended into my scene, fit easily into play furniture to play house.

Two houses down from where we lived, there was an empty half acre where a home once stood but now was overgrown with beautiful Queen Ann's Lace, milkweed, daisies, dark purple clover, and a deep back border of four feet tall single and double blossom hollyhocks. Everyone in the neighborhood called it The Old Lot: Ma, can I go play in the Old Lot? Where is Winthrop? He's in the Old Lot with Roy and Shurley. C'mon, Tish, let's go play in the Old Lot! There was a stand of burdock with leaves so large, we declared them African jungle plants and broke them off to swoop ceremoniously creating a breeze for Winthrop Tribal Chief seated on elegant stone throne that probably was an uncovered portion of porch foundation. Our notion of Africa was a combination of Edgar Rice Burroughs and *National Geographic.* Shurley's collection of *National Geographic* stood as tall as me and ran almost the length of his bedroom, without a subscription. Mother brought copies of *National Geographic* as a treat for Shurley in the same way she brought *Vogue, Bazaar The New Yorker, Esquire* and *Jack and Jill* magazines. From The Rum.

Our days had smooth room for slow-winding fantasy. Even housework with Mother moved along at the same pace. I do not like housework. Yet, I remember sitting under the dining room table as if we were in our own cozy play house as Tish and I worked dustcloths into the crevices of the carved table legs. Talk glided around, and my mother braided directions and storytelling together. Listen carefully, watch closely, work hard. Finish, check again. Carefully, to make sure it is done right. I learned the standard cautions from Mother before I read them in books, discovering that some tales were not hers alone, as I started reading beyond picture books. The Boy Who Cried Wolf when I had driven her to the brink, appearing again and again with whines of my big brothers' transgressions, Dog in the Manger since of course I had siblings that did not deserve any of my precious Tinkertoys or crayons; the Fox and the Grapes.

When spring cleaning came, there was no way to escape. Mother became organizing taskmaster. And everyone (of course not my father) scrubbed and polished, spinning all over the house. Spring cleaning in every house was hectic serious whirl. Curtains were pulled down, boiled with bluing, laundered, starched and placed on wooden frames called lace curtain stretchers. Cupboards scrubbed and reorganized, rugs hung across the backyard clothesline to be beaten with all your might until every particle of dust flew free. Walls scrubbed and furniture polished to shiny glow. Frantic dawn-to-dark cleaning went on for days. The whole house had to be bright and glistening for the season. This mad-dash cleansing was to set our house right for the year.

XIII

By the time spring turned into summer each year, the Old Lot became a meadow. Burdock, grass, yarrow and buttercups grew high enough to lie lost in. Wondrous weeds so thick and beautiful, looking up I could hardly see any sky. Joan. Joan. Joan? And when I didn't answer, Mother came to the edge of the Old Lot to call, and she could not find me anywhere. But I saw her, and loved staying very still, hiding.

My mother would leave. And we knew I was going to follow.

Baby Tish and Joan

Afterword
By Martha Southgate

You may have picked up this book because you heard about my mother's incredible journey through *In Their Path*. Or maybe you heard her speak. Or maybe you liked the picture on the cover—she was a beautiful little girl. Whatever made you pick it up, you probably laughed and cried as you read it. Laughed at the warmth and humor of her family life and cried at some of the horrible violence and abuse she lived through and with. But here's what my mother wants you to know now: "I hope the book makes it clear that the amnesia (about the abuse) allowed me to have a very good life."

'Bout Time was completed in 1998. Here's some of what's happened since. My mother continued to work on her recovery. The most spectacular and well-known part of this process was the journey that she began April 2002 at age 73, to cover a portion of the path of the Underground Railroad on foot. To use the language of her Web site: "She wanted to highlight the courage and resourcefulness of the American slave families and conductor families who risked so much for freedom on the Underground

Railroad. She called her journey IN THEIR PATH! and set out to increase awareness of a moment in history when people came together across color, creed and class to do freedom's work. Her journey has taken her on a 519-mile walk across Ohio and into Pennsylvania, New York and Canada. From schoolchildren to community groups, bank president to truck driver, her inspiring story and message of unity have resonated over the miles. Her walk has ended, but her mission continues." The walk and the attention and enthusiasm it engendered resonates to this day as my mother speaks and visits all over Ohio at schools and community and historical organizations, spreading the word about the Underground Railroad and the courageous men, women and children who were part of it.

My mother thought of her walk as a calling. From that calling she wanted to address the need to free ourselves from racism's bond of shame. For whites who, like Edward Ball in his award-winning book, *Slaves in the Family*, "... felt shame about the broken society that had washed up when the tide of slavery receded." And for blacks who may have absorbed the insidious, denigrating shame of racist enslavement. She says, "That is the universal shame I had in mind that I was going to walk free of. In my heart, this long, often solitary walk actually also freed me of the small lingering incest-shame I still carried after all those years. In the last couple of years (I'm not sure when) I looked back and realized that somewhere along the way I knew *he* was forgiven. Lovely."

When the walk ended, she founded Restore Cleveland Hope Inc. along with other dedicated activists. This grassroots non-profit organization successfully campaigned to save the Cozad-Bates House (11508 Mayfield Road), the only pre-Civil War home still standing in Cleveland's University Circle area. RCH Inc.'s ongoing mission is to establish an Underground Railroad Education and Resource Center within the house.

My mother now has nine grandchildren ranging in age from 3 to 15 living in New York City, Memphis, Atlanta and Cleveland. She is one of the busiest, most content people I know, so busy I can never get her on the phone. And so the blessings continue. People are always telling me that my mother is a remarkable woman. I have to agree. I'm honored to be her daughter.

Martha Southgate is the author of three novels, most recently Third Girl From the Left *(Houghton Mifflin) You can visit her Web site at* www.marthasouthgate.com.

For more information, visit www.intheirpath.org and www.restoreclevelandhope.org.

In Gratitude

    For love, wisdom, and joy from family and so many friends plus the thousands who inspired me along the Underground Railroad walk. I had so much, I have so much. I am so blessed. Thank you.

    Thank you to my entire family. My sister Letitia (Tish), my niece Gianna and her spouse Lauren. My grown children and their families: eldest daughter Martha and her husband Jeff, their children Nate and Ruby; son Robert and his wife Candy, their children Irene and Brian; daughter Letitia and her husband Shelley, their children Helena and Shelley Alexander; and son Dan, his stepdaughter Jocelyn, and sons Nik, Jeremy and Brandon.

    Thank you Cleveland Rape Crisis Center for healing help; Cleveland State University's Project 60 for getting me started as a writer; Ragdale Foundation's Frances Shaw Fellowship for early writing support; Charlotte's Web (Kathy, Marjorie and Fran) for continuing writing support; and Euclid Congregational Church and Restore Cleveland Hope Inc. for this wonderful possibility of the Beloved Community.

My family: big and small, short and taller, straight and gay, black, brown and white. Nine grandchildren.

All that is left of my growing-up family is Tish and me. I am five years older and four inches shorter so she often introduces me as her little sister, and I am again wrapped in the warmth of her love.

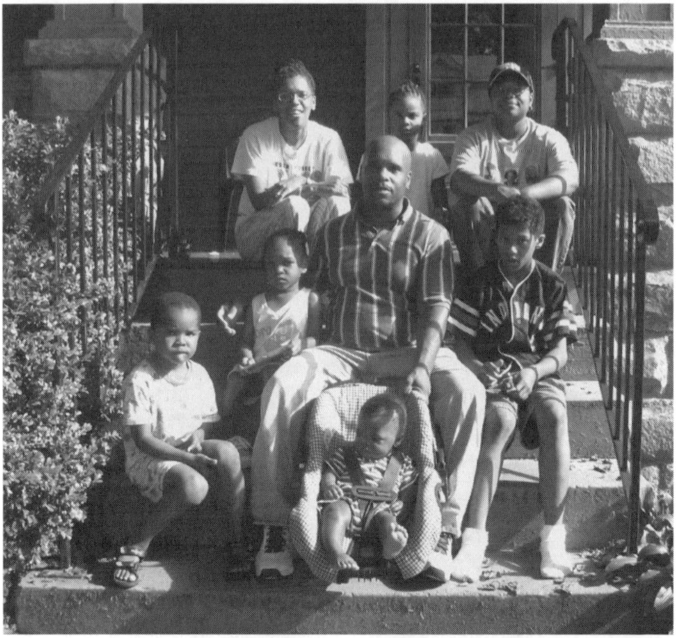

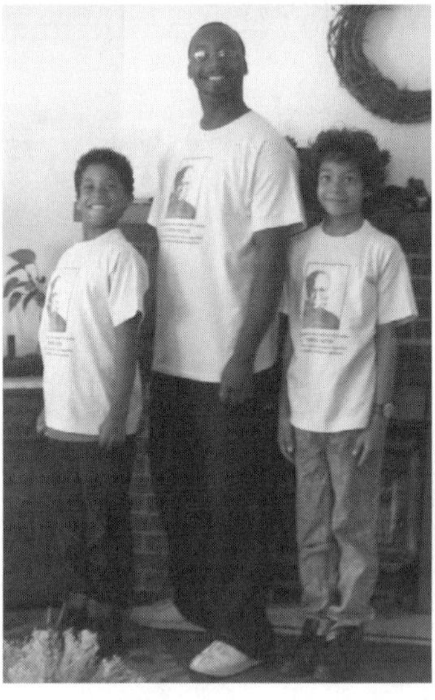

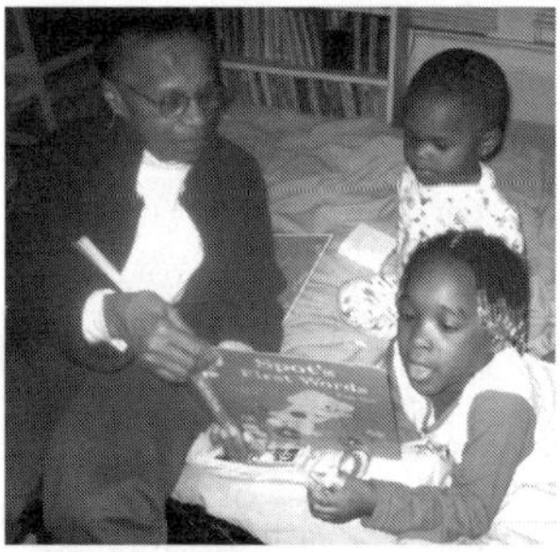

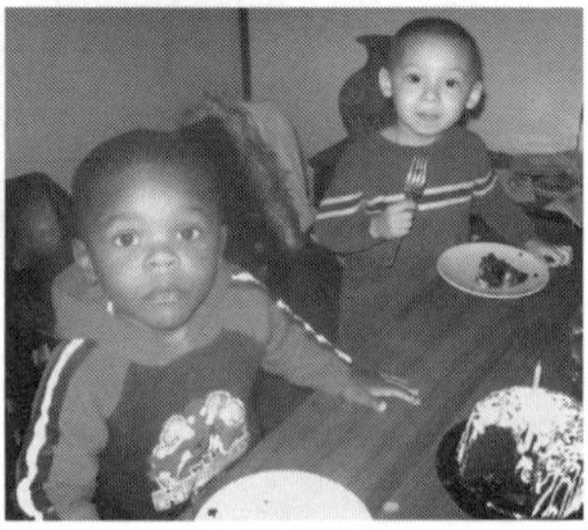

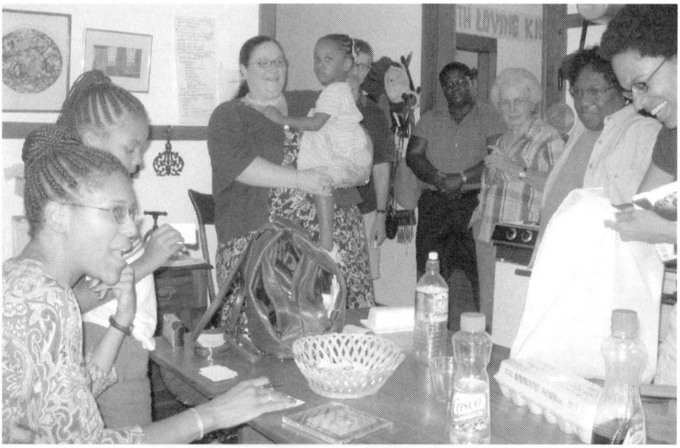

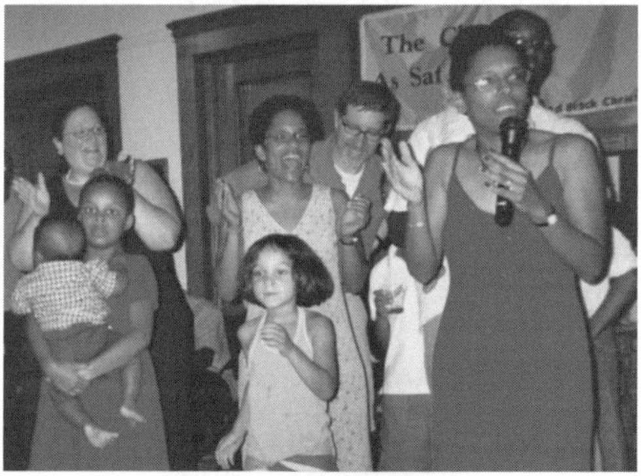

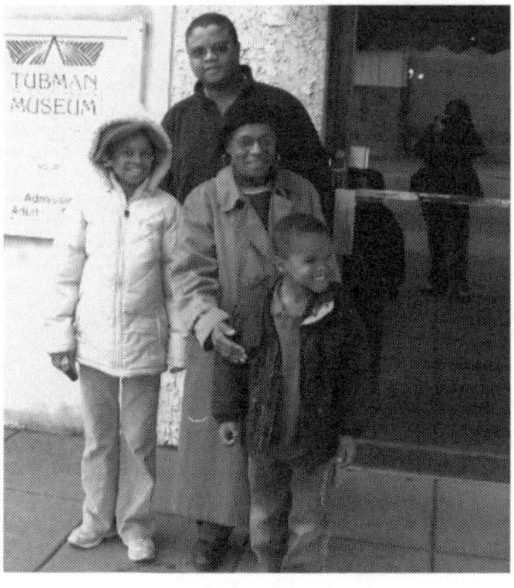
TUBMAN
MUSEUM

About the Author

Joan Southgate is a retired social worker, community organizer and founder of Restore Cleveland Hope Inc. She won Ragdale Foundation's 1996 Frances Shaw Fellowship. Her first book, In Their Path: A Grandmother's 519-mile Underground Railroad Walk, *chronicles her journey honoring the enslaved, the freedom seekers and the conductors and celebrates the many modern-day "conductors" who were drawn to her message of healing and hope.*

Visit www.restoreclevelandhope.org and www.intheirpath.org for more information.

Learn about Joan Southgate's journey across
Ohio and on to Canada. Available for sale at
www.intheirpath.org.